The Tao *of* Daily Life

JEREMY P. TARCHER/PENGUIN

a member of Penguin Group (USA) Inc.

New York

The Tao *of* Daily Life

The Mysteries of the Orient Revealed • *The Joys of Inner Harmony Found*

The Path to Enlightenment Illuminated

DEREK LIN

JEREMY P. TARCHER/PENGUIN
Published by the Penguin Group
Penguin Group (USA) Inc., 375 Hudson Street, New York, New York 10014, USA • Penguin Group (Canada),
90 Eglinton Avenue East, Suite 700, Toronto, Ontario M4P 2Y3, Canada (a division of Pearson Penguin
Canada Inc.) • Penguin Books Ltd, 80 Strand, London WC2R 0RL, England • Penguin Ireland,
25 St Stephen's Green, Dublin 2, Ireland (a division of Penguin Books Ltd) • Penguin Group (Australia),
250 Camberwell Road, Camberwell, Victoria 3124, Australia (a division of Pearson Australia Group Pty Ltd) •
Penguin Books India Pvt Ltd, 11 Community Centre, Panchsheel Park, New Delhi–110 017, India •
Penguin Group (NZ), 67 Apollo Drive, Rosedale, North Shore 0745, Auckland, New Zealand (a division
of Pearson New Zealand Ltd) • Penguin Books (South Africa) (Pty) Ltd, 24 Sturdee Avenue, Rosebank,
Johannesburg 2196, South Africa

Penguin Books Ltd, Registered Offices: 80 Strand, London WC2R 0RL, England

Most Tarcher/Penguin books are available at special quantity discounts for bulk purchase for sales promotions,
premiums, fund-raising, and educational needs. Special books or book excerpts also can be created to fit specific
needs. For details, write Penguin Group (USA) Inc. Special Markets, 375 Hudson Street, New York, NY 10014.

Library of Congress Cataloging-in-Publication Data

Lin, Derek, date.
The Tao of daily life : the mysteries of the Orient revealed : the joys of inner harmony found :
the path to enlightenment illuminated / Derek Lin.
p.   cm.
ISBN 978-1-58542-583-9
1. Tao.   I. Title.
B127.T3L53   2007   2007013647
299.5'1444—dc22

Printed in the United States of America
1   3   5   7   9   10   8   6   4   2

This book is printed on acid-free paper. ♾

BOOK DESIGN BY NICOLE LAROCHE

While the author has made every effort to provide accurate telephone numbers and Internet addresses at the time
of publication, neither the publisher nor the author assumes any responsibility for errors, or for changes that occur
after publication. Further, the publisher does not have any control over and does not assume any responsibility
for author or third-party websites or their content.

This book is dedicated to Janice.

Contents

PART TWO

At Work

PART THREE

With Friends

PART FOUR

With Family

PART FIVE

At Night

The Tao *of* Daily Life

Introduction

The *Tao* is Chinese for "the path" or "the way," and this book is your invitation to a journey on the Tao. It is a journey of discovery, where you gain not only timeless wisdom, but also insights about yourself and your life.

The Tao is incredibly ancient. Many people who know something about it will tell you that the philosophy began about 2,500 years ago, but the Tao is actually much older than that. It dates back at least to the time of Huangdi, the mythical emperor who ruled China more than 4,600 years ago.

There is one simple reason for the Tao to have survived through the ages intact: it works. The principles of the Tao are extremely effective when applied to life. The philosophy as a whole is nothing less than a practical, useful guide to living life in a way that is smooth, peaceful, and full of energy.

The purpose of this book is to present the secrets of the Tao in the most accessible way imaginable—via stories. Throughout the history of China, sages and masters have learned and taught the Tao by hearing and telling stories, generation after generation. By taking a journey on the Tao, you have become part of this great oral tradition.*

As you absorb these stories and make use of their wisdom, you will begin to notice changes in your life. You will become more composed and more at ease in various situations; you will be able to handle challenges and difficulties with less effort and better results. The more you practice the Tao, the more you will see how marvelously powerful it really is.

You will come to realize that your journey on the Tao is, in many ways, the most worthwhile exploration you can undertake. You will be able to see your life in a new light, and observe everything around you with a clarity as never before. You may even feel compelled to continue the tradition by sharing the stories with others so they can also explore their own Tao of daily life.

All of the above and more await you. Come, let us embark together.

*All *Tao Te Ching* translations quoted herein are from the author's original work published in 2006 as *Tao Te Ching: Annotated & Explained.*

PART ONE

In the Morning

清晨

The beginning of a new day is a wondrous gift. It is a blank page, containing nothing and yet filled with possibilities. It is the perfect time to prime yourself for the unknown challenges ahead by contemplating the Tao and reminding yourself to practice the following throughout the day:

- *Live fully in the here and now.*
- *Appreciate the simple things in life.*
- *Take responsibility for the unfolding of your destiny.*

To put yourself in the right frame of mind, it can be very helpful to consider the following questions:

- *How will I move forward in my life journey today?*
- *How will I remain in tune with the Tao today?*

Chapter 1

Fish in the Ocean

What Is This Thing Called Tao?

海中之魚

Once upon a time, a young fish asked an old fish: "Everyone talks about this thing called 'ocean.' What exactly is it?"

The older and wiser fish answered: "The ocean is that which surrounds you on all sides."

The younger fish didn't understand: "What do you mean? There is nothing around me! If the ocean surrounds me on all sides, why can I not see it?"

"Of course you cannot," the old fish said patiently. "The ocean is both inside and outside of you. When you move, it moves with you; when you stop, it stops as well. You were born in the ocean and you will die in it. It wraps itself around you, just as your own skin does."

"But how can I tell it exists, if I cannot see it?"

"You must use more than your eyes. We may not be able see the ocean, but we can definitely feel it. Trust your feelings—they are the key."

The Tao
道

Confucius once said: "Fish forget they live in water; people forget they live in the Tao." The Tao is the invisible ocean that surrounds us on all sides. It permeates everything at every level of existence, so it is both inside and outside of us. It enfolds us like our own skin, and yet we cannot perceive it with our physical senses.

The *Tao* is Chinese for "the path" or "the way," but it is also much more than the literal meaning. Sages have attempted to explain the Tao in the following ways:

- *Whatever the ultimate principle is that underlies reality, we call it the Tao.*
- *Whatever the one truth is at the center of all spiritual truths, that is the Tao.*

- *Whatever the universal source of consciousness is, we will give it the name Tao.*
- *Whatever the force is that is ultimately responsible for moving everything in the universe—from galaxies to human beings to subatomic particles—that force is what we call the Tao.*

These are only approximations. No one understands the Tao completely, and it is beyond the power of words to describe or define. We live in the Tao and move within it every day, but like the fish in the ocean, we are barely aware of its existence. Once in a while we may catch a glimpse—we get the feeling that there is some power behind the scenes, some intelligence coordinating everything—but the feeling is fleeting.

The only way we can approach the Tao is to relax the death grip of logic, and engage the far more powerful tool of intuition. When the rationality of the brain utterly fails to grasp the Tao, the heart will step in to embrace it with a way of knowing that is beyond knowledge. Feeling is the key.

道也者，不可須臾離也；可離，非道也。

Chapter 2

Living in the Moment

Being Mindful in the Present

活在當下

One day, while walking through the wilderness, a man encountered a vicious tiger. He ran for his life, and the tiger gave chase.

The man came to the edge of a cliff, and the tiger was almost upon him. Having no choice, he held on to a vine with both hands and climbed down.

Halfway down the cliff, the man looked up and saw the tiger at the top, baring its fangs. He looked down and saw another tiger at the bottom, waiting for his arrival and roaring at him. He was caught between the two.

Two rats, one white and one black, showed up on the vine above him. As if he didn't have enough to worry about, they started gnawing on the vine.

He knew that as the rats kept gnawing, they would reach a point when the vine *would no longer be able to support his weight. It would break and he would fall. He tried to shoo the rats away, but they kept coming back.*

At that moment, he noticed a strawberry growing on the face of the cliff, not far away from him. It looked plump and ripe. Holding on to the vine with one hand and reaching out with the other, he plucked it.

With a tiger above, another below, and two rats continuing to gnaw on his vine, the man tasted the strawberry and found it absolutely delicious.

The Tao

道

Despite his perilous situation, the man chose not to let unrealized dangers paralyze him. He was able to seize the moment and savor it.

The top of the cliff represents the past. It's where the man had been and where he came from. In terms of your personal timeline, this metaphor refers to all of your experiences and memories from the life that you have already lived.

Climbing up the vine, toward the top of the cliff, would be to revisit the past. The tiger at the top represents the danger of dwelling in the past too much. If we constantly beat ourselves up for not being able to do certain things as well as we should, or if we wallow in regret and shame over mistakes we have made, then the tiger has wounded us with its sharp claws. If we cannot let go of negative experiences from the past that make us timid and afraid, or if we feel like victims because we come from a traumatic or perhaps abusive background, then the tiger has taken a painful bite out of us.

The tiger also represents the impossibility of going back in time to fix something. Sometimes we wish we could turn back the clock and do certain things over. Perhaps you think of the perfect comeback long after the right moment has passed; perhaps there was a special someone from high school that you should have approached but didn't; perhaps you said something hurtful to a loved one and would do anything to take it back. Unfortunately, the pathway of time is a one-way street—the fearsome tiger guards the top of the cliff, and mere mortals may not pass.

The bottom of the cliff represents the future. It is the undiscovered country, the unwritten chapter. The future contains all of your dreams and fears, aspirations and disappointments, potential victories and possible setbacks. It is the mysterious and uncertain domain of tomorrow.

Climbing down the vine, closer to the bottom of the cliff, is to look ahead, anticipate and speculate about the future. The tiger at the bottom represents the danger of being excessively concerned about that which is yet to come—particularly at the expense of our ability to act, or to maintain peace of mind.

Many of us have had the experience of worrying endlessly about an upcoming performance, speech, or job interview. We think about all the things that can go wrong. We cannot get a good night's sleep because we're too nervous about the next day.

So what happens when the event comes around? Our inability to relax disconnects us from the creative genius of the Tao. We are not able to be at our best. We cannot channel all that nervous energy into effective action; instead, it turns right into tension and stress. We have climbed too low on the vine and gotten too close to the tiger, thus allowing it to cause us damage.

The tiger at the bottom also represents the ultimate finality of death. Death waits patiently for all of us in the future. It knows that sooner or later we will be within its grasp. When the tiger roars up at us, we feel the chilling winds of mortality.

The man's position between the two tigers represents the present. Note that he hangs suspended in midair. In the same way, we too live suspended between the past and the future.

This thing we call "now" or "the present instant" can be quite an elusive concept. As soon as you point to an instant and define it as "now," it slips past your finger and is no longer the present. Another instant, equally elusive, takes its place. No matter how hard you try, you will never be able to pin it down.

The present also defies definition, just like the Tao. Even though we can measure time with great accuracy, our technical precision gives us no help at all in isolating that infinitesimal slice of zero-duration time. Although we have the technology to build an atomic clock with an error margin of less than ten billionths of a second, all the atomic clocks in the world cannot capture the magic of the present instant.

Although an instant of time is beyond our grasp, the paradox of existence is that the present is what we do have. Indeed, it is all we ever have. You can never have the past or the future; one is irretrievably gone and the other is yet to come. The present is here and now, and it is yours completely and unconditionally. No one can take it away from you, and you alone have the power to decide how to use it.

The vine represents life in the material world. Just as the man holds on to the vine with both hands, we too cling to physical life stubbornly. Our survival instincts compel us to literally hold on for dear life, and we won't let go without a struggle.

Climbing down the vine isn't an optional activity. The man, chased by the tiger, has no choice but to climb down. Similarly, once we are born into this

world, we have no choice but to live out our lives from one moment t[...]
Thus, the vine can also be seen as the main component of *samsara*—t[...]
of birth and death.

The two rats represent the passage of time. They are black and white in col[...]
for the simple reason that they symbolize day and night.

The rats gnaw on the vine, making it weaker and weaker. This represents how
each cycle of day and night brings us a little closer to death. When the vine
breaks, the man plummets toward certain doom. In the same way, when a suf-
ficient number of days and nights have passed, the physical life we cling to will
be broken, and it will be time for the ultimate finality of death. We will have
no choice but to confront the tiger.

Just as the man tries to shoo the rats away, we try to forestall aging and keep
disease at bay. We have entire industries devoted to various measures to keep us
young and healthy or, at the very least, to maintain the appearance of youth and
health. Consider all the vitamins, supplements, treatments, health spas, hor-
mone replacement therapies, face lifts, liposuction, hair transplants, all manners
of implants . . . the list goes on.

But just as the rats keep coming back, time marches ever onward and slows
down for no one. Despite our best efforts, our time in this mortal plane remains limited.

stounding beauty, bliss, energy, and vitality

there, always available for those who have

ommunion with nature. Bear silent wit-

erceive reality as an endless interplay of

ll as within you. From the macrocos-

al processes go about their business,

gence far beyond our grasp.

uch beauty and goodness in each present moment and the in-

instant, that if you were to take in too much at once, you would be hopelessly overwhelmed. In the language of our story, we might say that the strawberry is full of incredibly delicious juice.

To pluck the strawberry is to seize the moment. When you do so, you are being mindful of the present, directing your attention to the flow that moves through you, and choosing to immerse fully in the river of the eternal now.

To taste the strawberry is to fully savor the flavor of reality. When you do so, you begin to appreciate the miracle of existence and notice a beauty that is ever present no matter where you look. This fills your heart with gladness and gratitude.

Plucking and tasting the strawberry may be much easier said than done.

Most of the time, most of us have trouble tapping into the powerful state of mindfulness that allows us to seize the moment and savor reality. There are obstacles that get in the way.

The first obstacle, which most Tao cultivators have overcome, is the lack of awareness. Many people live each day mired in the past or worried about the future, unaware of the treasure of the present that they already possess. In terms of the story, it is as if the man is so busy looking up and down that he never notices the succulent fruit right next to him.

The second obstacle is more difficult, and most of us encounter it from time to time. Consider a scenario where the man sees the strawberry, but because he's too concerned about the tiger above and fearful of the tiger below, he has no appetite. Although he knows quite well where the strawberry is, he has no interest in getting it.

Someone who is faced with this obstacle may say, "It's great to understand the metaphors in the story, but there's a difference between that and putting the understanding into actual practice. I can see now that my goal should be to live in the moment, but how exactly do I do that?"

The story offers a clue. When the man saw the strawberry, he held on to the vine with one hand and reached out with the other. This action incorporates two essential elements: letting go and reaching out.

The man could not pluck the strawberry if he insisted on holding on with both hands. With both hands gripping the vine tightly, all he could do would be to stare at it. In order to get the prize, he needed to relax one hand and detach it from the vine.

It is exactly the same with life. The vine represents our physical existence on this material plane. Holding on to it tightly is equivalent to having strong attachments to material concerns. With such attachments, you cannot let go. This is a surefire way to prevent you from enjoying the present.

It sounds simple when we talk about it like this, but think of the people you know who are so focused on making and saving money that they never take the time to enjoy life. If you observe them you'll see that they cannot relax even when they go through the motions. For instance, when they take a vacation, they cannot stop thinking about the office. In the language of our story, such people have a death grip on the vine.

I know of a gentleman whose attachment was the stock market. He was a day trader who watched the market minute by minute. When friends talked to him on the phone, they could always tell when his stock symbols scrolled across the electronic ticker tape, because his replies would suddenly become much slower as he pretended to be listening. This was a clear case in which his strong attachment to material concerns completely blocked his ability to enjoy conversations with old friends—one of the best things in life.

The other element, equally important, is to reach out, to explore. The comfort zone may be comfortable, but it also offers nothing new. In order to get the strawberry, you need to venture beyond the familiar, to probe for a prize that is within sight but not quite within grasp.

The Tao manifests itself in life, and the characteristic of life is that it grows. Life is constantly exploring new territories, taking chances, and going places it hasn't been before. If we do the same, we will quickly find that life is fresh and exciting and full of possibilities. We will see that living in the present is both easy and exhilarating.

Thus, our story teaches that when we have trouble living fully and mindfully in the moment, we only need to ask ourselves questions like the following:

- *What are my attachments? What are some things I cannot let go? What attachments am I willing to release, in order to live life to the fullest?*
- *Am I learning anything new? Meeting new people? Doing anything I haven't done before? What might be some fun subjects that I can study? What might be some interesting projects I can tackle?*

Your answers to questions like these will point out the path you should follow. Formulate your plans accordingly.

As you follow your plan of action to live mindfully in the moment, you will find it easier and easier to stop dwelling in the past or worrying excessively about the future. As you enjoy the present more and more, you will also find that unpleasant or even painful memories no longer affect you; concerns or even fears about future uncertainties no longer paralyze you.

You will find that the present is literally a wonderful present. It is a miraculous gift filled with peace, contentment, energy, and excitement. It is a box full of delicious strawberries.

You begin to realize that the only requirement to be deserving of such a gift is that you accept it and enjoy it. You are amazed that there are people who cannot receive it. Some do not even realize it is being offered to them. They do not recognize it as their birthright, nor do they understand its incredible value.

You collect your thoughts back into yourself. It is time to unwrap your own present.

珍惜生命，把握當下。

Chapter 3

The Best Meal

Finding Joy in the Simple Things

最好的一餐

In 1900, toward the end of the Ch'ing dynasty, China found itself in discord and turmoil. European countries had made their entrance. They easily dominated the scene with their superior technology and firepower. Anti-foreign Chinese militants fought back, even though they were hopelessly outgunned.

The conflict escalated until Beijing itself turned into the battleground. The situation became more and more dangerous until it was no longer prudent for Empress Tz'u-hsi to remain in the palace. Escorted by imperial guards and personal servants, she fled into the countryside.

Fear and uncertainty gripped the dowager empress. What was happening to her palace? Her city? Her country? Never in her sixty-five years had Tz'u-hsi felt so vul-

nerable. It seemed as if the violence they left behind in Beijing might pounce on them at any moment, threatening even her personal safety.

Days later, they came upon a farming village, and decided to get some much-needed rest. After her seemingly endless, fearful flight, Tz'u-hsi was physically exhausted, emotionally drained, and ravenously hungry. She ordered that food be brought forth at once.

The farmers prepared a meal with the best they had, which wasn't much. They were much too poor to have anything beyond the bare necessities. After much scrounging, they came up with rice porridge and a dish of preserved snails.

To Tz'u-hsi, the meal was incredibly delicious. She went for seconds, and then thirds. She had never tasted such delicacies all her life. Curious, she asked: "What do you call these marvelous dishes?"

The farmers knew the meal was the most common imaginable, without any class or artistic distinctions. But even in times of distress, anything the empress touched had to be appropriate to her exalted station.

"Um . . . Your Majesty had pearl soup and stewed phoenix eyes," they told her.

Empress Tz'u-hsi thought of the cuisine at the palace. Every meal was an elaborate banquet, featuring a hundred and twenty entrées, all painstakingly prepared by imperial chefs. Even though these chefs were the best in all of China, none of their culinary creations satisfied her appetite as this remarkable meal she just had.

Later, after the fighting subsided, Tz'u-hsi was finally able to return to the palace. Safely ensconced in opulent seclusion, she reflected upon her ordeal. She recalled the pearl soup and the stewed phoenix eyes and wanted to have them again, but much to her annoyance, the imperial chefs swore they had never heard of such things.

The Tao

道

The dowager empress never figured out the secret. Her chefs were peerless in terms skills and talent, but even they could not give her the one crucial element she needed: hunger. She was the only one who could create for herself this magical ingredient, this ultimate sauce that made any food incredibly delicious.

This is a good illustration of *p'u,* the Tao principle of simplicity. Just like the empress in the palace, you and I live in a world of elaborate complexities. The one hundred and twenty entrées are the numerous materialistic attractions, distractions, and temptations offered to us every day. As we partake in these intricately prepared delights, our senses become increasingly numb. Our appetites become jaded, and we wonder: Whatever happened to the joie de vivre? Where is that old zest for life?

This is exactly what Lao Tzu talks about in chapter 12 of *Tao Te Ching:*

The five colors make one blind in the eyes
The five sounds make one deaf in the ears
The five flavors make one tasteless in the mouth

The five colors, sounds, and flavors are not positive or negative in themselves. They can quickly become negative, though, if we pursue them blindly and neglect the important basics of life. When that happens, we stray from the path of moderation and move against the flow of Tao.

This seems to happen quite a bit in this day and age, perhaps because the modern world bombards us with so many sensory stimuli. It becomes easy for us to forget about the joys of simplicity. Perhaps we need to remind ourselves of our fundamental, simplistic nature through a number of examples.

Consider the fact that we are surrounded by an incredible variety of beverages. At any given moment we can be drinking wine, beer, juice, soda, punch, tea, milk, coffee, hot cocoa . . . the list goes on. Each type of beverage contains its own bewildering array of flavors and variations. Put them all together, and you've got hundreds of different drinks, all designed to appeal to the taste buds.

Despite all that, when you really need liquid, when you're hot and thirsty—perhaps after jogging or working out—nothing beats water, the most delicious beverage of all. We can all remember a time, probably not long ago, when we drank plain water deeply and felt absolutely amazing and totally invigorated.

Water can do that to us without anything being added to it. There is no sugar, caffeine, or flavoring in it. It is not made from concentrates, there's no powder to mix, you don't need to carbonate it with compressed gas. It doesn't need to be homogenized, pasteurized, or fermented. In order to get it, we don't need oak barrels, bottling plants, breweries, or stills. It is just water, the essence of simplicity and the ultimate drink.

Let's also consider the way we take ourselves places. We all enjoy the convenience of ubiquitous transportation in the modern world. Whether you drive your own car, take the bus, or ride the train, the fact is that human beings can get around more easily and quickly than at any time in history.

We're not limited to the ground either. Nowadays we can fly to business conferences or take a cruise to exotic destinations for a vacation. We can go farther and cover larger areas; we can travel to almost any spot in the world if we really want to.

At the same time that we zip from one place to another at high speeds, simple, everyday walking is becoming a lost art. We no longer recall what a subtle yet enduring pleasure walking can be, so we do it less and less.

That's a pity, because there is nothing quite like walking to harmonize the flow of energy throughout your entire being. Walking moves you closer to optimal health like no other exercise.

You can prove this to yourself simply by taking a walk outside for half an hour. When you get back in the house, pay attention to exactly how you feel. You will find yourself in a pleasant and renewed mental state, and you will sense a force circulating inside and outside of your body.

If you start out the walk tense and stressed, you will be relaxed by the end of it—try closing and opening your hands to check your state of relaxation. If you start out in a blue mood, by the end of the walk your outlook will be much brighter. If you start out with an incipient headache, by the end of the walk it will have disappeared. Compare these feelings to the way you feel when you come home after fighting through traffic.

The feeling of well-being and optimal health that walking gives you has been confirmed by medical science. Several studies have shown that walking cuts down one's risk of cancer and heart disease dramatically. Walking even lowers the risk of diabetes *by half.* That's something no known medicine can do. Euphoric medical researchers have taken to calling walking "the miracle cure."

Note that walking delivers these benefits without requiring anything except your own two feet. You don't need a license, a ticket, insurance, or gasoline. You won't get cut off when attempting to change lanes or get pulled over for speeding. When you reconnect with the simple pleasure of walking, you'll wonder how you ever managed to neglect this fundamental, essential aspect of life.

When we discuss p'u, you know we have to touch on the colorful sights and sounds of the modern world. We are blessed with an astounding variety of entertainment. At any given moment we can choose to listen to the radio, music CDs, or iPods. If we want visuals, we can watch TV, DVDs, or videotapes.

With TV, we may decide to view a news broadcast, a sitcom, a game show, a police drama, a soap opera, a documentary, sports . . . the list goes on. If there's nothing good on TV (as often seems to be the case), we can go out to see a play, attend a concert, or perhaps catch a movie.

We have so many options, it is mind-boggling. As a result, people seem to overdose on entertainment. I know a fellow who used to spend his entire weekend in the movie cinema at a local mall. He would get in on the early show and then sneak from one theater to the next, eventually seeing all the movies for the price of one. He did this because he was lonesome and miserable.

Not all of us have done the above, but many of us have done something similar. Think of the last time you vegetated on the couch, flipping from one channel to the next, feeling profoundly bored and yet unable to break away. In more ways than one, the couch potato is but a different version of the lonely figure moving furtively from one movie to another.

Consider the amount of work and technology that go into the production of entertainment today, and it seems incredible that all the dazzling cinematography and high-fidelity digital sound serve only to numb us even more. And yet it is precisely because we have become jaded that the entertainment industry cranks up the violence and gore, just to give us a stronger dose of excitement and stimulation.

Again, all of this happens because we tend to disconnect ourselves from simplicity. We forget all about the wonder and beauty of the basic things in life.

We forget about the spectacular sunset, the glorious full moon, the angelic smile of an infant, or the glimmer of a soul when you look deeply into your lover's eyes. These are the simplest things imaginable, and yet beautiful beyond description. No Hollywood special effects will ever be able to replace them.

We forget about golden, blessed silence. We forget about the treasured moments when you can hear yourself think, or quiet your thoughts and relax into wordless communion with the Tao.

Silence plays for you the song of serenity and the sounds of stillness without speakers or subwoofers, CD players or iPods, microphones or musical instruments. What is melody after all, but a series of notes framing the space between them? Perhaps it is as rock star Sting says: silence may well be the ultimate music.

When you think about it this way, and reflect back on water and walking, you begin to see that the basic things in life can indeed be more powerful than the most elaborate human constructs. This is the principle of p'u.

We have seen that the power of simplicity was greater than the will of Empress Tz'u-hsi. Even though she wielded absolute power, she could not bend the laws of nature. If she wished to experience the joy of simplicity, she had to reduce complexity in her life. Because she could not do that, the pearl soup and stewed phoenix eyes would be forever lost to her. No imperial decree could ever change that.

Now that you understand this, you can see that what you have grasped—spiritual truth—is at a level beyond the absolute power of an absolute ruler. If you hold on to this simple truth and apply it, you will capture without effort something beyond value, something that eluded the empress a hundred years ago:

The ability to truly savor life . . . with relish and gusto!

五色令人目盲，五音令人耳聾，五味令人口爽。

Chapter 4
The Monk and the Spider

Taking Responsibility for Your Destiny

和尚與蜘蛛

Once upon a time, there was a monk who had trouble meditating. Whenever he tried going into meditation, a giant spider would appear. No matter what he did, he could not get rid of it.

At his wit's end, the monk sought help from his master. The master instructed him to prepare a brush at his side for the next attempt. When the spider appeared again, he was to use the brush to draw a circle on it.

The monk followed these instructions and attempted meditation. Sure enough, the giant spider came back. The monk followed the plan and drew a circle on the monster. As soon as he did so, the spider disappeared, and he was able to resume meditation in peace.

When he withdrew from the meditative state, the first thing he saw was a big black circle on his own belly. His worst enemy had been himself—exactly as the master had expected.

The Tao
道

One of the significant insights in the Tao is that many of the problems we encounter in life come from the mind within, rather than the external world. To solve such problems, we need to stop blaming outside forces that we have no control over, and instead take a long hard look at ourselves. When we realize that we are the cause of our own misfortunes, we can begin to adjust our thinking at a fundamental level, and start to create real changes.

There is a true story that illustrates this teaching beautifully. At a football game in Monterey Park, California, several people became ill from food poisoning. The doctor who diagnosed them found that they all drank soft drinks from one particular vending machine, so he thought that the machine must be the cause. Acting quickly to prevent more illness, he relayed this information to the announcer, who in turn announced it over the loudspeakers.

Almost immediately panic broke out in the stadium when some people realized that they, too, had bought sodas from the same machine. They threw up or passed out or felt terrible, further convincing everyone around them that the vending machine was at fault. Ambulances and paramedics transported these people to a nearby hospital, in a scene of utter chaos and confusion.

Later, upon further analysis, the doctor realized that the original problem was caused by something else, and not the soft drinks from the vending machine after all. So the people who were transported to the hospital really got sick over nothing!

Furthermore, when word of this discovery got to the hospital, it had an immediate impact on the newly admitted patients. They reacted at first with disbelief, then grudging acceptance, and finally complete recovery. Their symptoms disappeared into thin air and they walked out of the hospital soon thereafter.

In this true story, we see how a belief can strongly affect the physical world—in this case the bodies of the football fans. Was their illness any less real because the cause was imaginary? Their vomit certainly seemed real and smelled real to the cleaning crew! If the doctor continued to believe that the soft drink was the cause, and no one found out the truth, would they not continue to feel sick?

Perhaps this is a lesson to us about the power of the mind. It is a power that all of us possess yet few of us use. It can cause us harm and misery, or do our bidding and solve our problems. It all depends on our recognition of this truth, and what we decide to do with it.

Let us all examine our lives with this teaching in mind. Are our problems really things we cannot control? Or do they merely seem that way? What did we do or fail to do to allow these problems into our lives? Do we already have the power to solve them? Do we already hold the key without realizing it?

夫人神好清，而心擾之；人心好靜，而慾牽之。

Chapter 5

The Giant Peng Bird

Taking Flight on Your Great Spiritual Journey

鵬程萬里

In the desolate Northern Sea there is a fish. Its name is Kun. The size of the Kun is thousands of miles long. No one knows exactly how big it is.

The Kun transforms into a bird. The name of this bird is Peng. The size of the Peng is so great that no one knows exactly how large it is. Its incredible wingspan is thousands of miles wide.

The ocean begins to heave when the great winds blow across the waves. The might of this powerful wind is such that it allows even the Peng bird to take flight.

The giant Peng spreads its massive wings and splashes water to a height of three thousand miles. These wings generate a hurricane force, allowing the Peng to ride it up toward the sky until it is ninety thousand miles above the ocean.

The Peng is in full flight. Its wings are like the clouds that hang from the sky. Its destination is the Southern Sea—the heavenly ocean of brightness.

Way down below, a cicada and a little bird laugh at the giant Peng flying overhead. The little bird says: "Look at me, I fly all out and stop when I get to a tree. Sometimes I can't fly up quite so high and have to drop down to the ground. What's the use of rising up ninety thousand miles and then flying toward the Southern Sea?"

The Tao

道

This is the majestic beginning of the *Chuang Tzu*, a masterpiece of Chinese literature. It paints a stirring image of a mythical creature springing into action.

The Kun represents your soul in an initial, untapped state. The massive size of the Kun refers to the tremendous potential you possess. The Northern Sea is where you start out. It is a cold and dismal place, and you cannot see much in its murky depths. You are literally in the dark, swimming blindly. You are limited and, in a sense, trapped.

There are other fish in the Northern Sea as well, but they are much smaller. These are creatures that live a mundane existence, not suspecting that there is a greater world beyond the water. They have not glimpsed, as you have, this thing called the sky. In time, some of them will grow larger too, and begin to take an interest in the strange realm above the ocean. For the time being, you are the only one.

Then, one day, it happens. There is a breakthrough. The Kun undergoes a magical transformation. The soul has attained critical mass, triggering a spiritual chain reaction. The transformation is a fundamental change, rather than a mere accretion in size, as before. Scales become feathers; fins become wings. The nature of the soul changes, as do the rules that apply to it.

The effect is irreversible: the Kun can turn into the Peng, but not the other way around. Once the soul has attained adulthood it does not regress back into childhood. An irrevocable understanding has dawned upon you, and you know things will never be the same again.

This massive metamorphosis happens for a reason, and that is to prepare the Peng for its great journey. You will be flying toward the Southern Sea, the place of light and warmth. This journey represents your sacred task in life. It may be a quest for a higher level of spiritual development; it may be a personal mission to give of your love to the utmost; it may be a call to reach out to others and connect with them across vast interpersonal chasms. Whatever it is, your journey toward the heavenly ocean requires you to commit to something other than yourself and greater than yourself. This commitment is the true mark of virtue and an infinite source of personal fulfillment.

Then the opportunity comes. The great winds blow and the Peng surges into flight. This is your soul transcending its previous limits and boundaries. The Peng rises high above the ocean, no longer bound by the water. You experience a sense of freedom and a burst of energy. You have broken out of your constraints; you have stepped outside the box.

The winds of opportunity are the global megatrends affecting our lives in ways seen and unseen. We live in a historical nexus where advanced communication and transportation bring the East and the West closer and closer every day. The fusion of the two produces a synergy of tremendous power. The wind is picking up speed and moving across the entire world. The time for the journey is fast approaching.

The flight of the Peng is an awe-inspiring sight, its great speed matched only by its high altitude. It is so far above that when it looks down, the world seems to disappear into a blue expanse. Everything fades into the hazy distance.

When you take flight on your personal journey, one of the things that changes irrevocably is your perspective. Your sacred task confers upon you an expanded view of life. You see farther and your thinking tends to be long term. This is because greater plans require greater vision, and your aspirations have elevated far beyond the pedestrian. From that vantage point, the petty struggles of daily life simply do not have the same significance they once had.

The cicada and the little bird are those who simply cannot understand your goals or your motivation. As you continue your journey, you will encounter many like them. They are still mired in the material world. Their concerns are small and immediate and have more to do with struggling through another day so they can go home and assume the couch potato position.

The perspective of the cicada and the little bird is limited. They give little thought to greater spiritual issues and, should the subject ever come up, respond with a programmed script of platitudes. This is, quite literally, as high as they can fly. If you ask too much of them, they will only fall back down to the ground. If and when they acquire the same perception and can see what you see, they will understand why you do what you do. Until then, expect puzzlement, perhaps even ridicule.

Where are you in the great journey? Some of you may already be in flight, well on your way to the Southern Sea. Some of you are waiting for the right moment to surge into flight. The rest of you, perhaps most of you, are still swimming blindly in the Northern Sea, your massive potential untapped.

The journey beckons, great Kun. Are you ready for your transformation?

天行健，君子以自強不息。

Chapter 6
The Music of Heaven

Listening to the Universal Symphony of the Tao

天籟之聲

Nanguo Ziqi sat leaning against a table. He tilted his head back, breathed deeply, and entered into a state that transcended the self. His disciple Ziyou asked: "The stilled body can be like dry wood; can the stilled mind be like burnt ash? You seem very different today, Master. Why?"

Ziqi answered, "Good question! Today I have discarded my egocentric perspective. Do you understand what I mean? You've heard the music of people, but not the music of earth. And if you have heard the music of earth, you haven't heard the music of heaven!"

Ziyou said, "Please tell me about this music, Master."

Ziqi said, "When the great earth breathes, we call it wind. When the wind blows, all the holes in nature roar with sound. Have you not heard the howling? Look at the trees on the mountain, the big old trees with the numerous openings, like nostrils, like mouths, like ears, like sockets, like pens, like grindstones, like deep pools, like shallow ponds. They sound like water rushing forth, arrows shot out, scolding, inhaling, yelling, screaming, laughing, sighing. Initially the wind sings one note; what follows sings another note to harmonize. Gentle breeze whispers softly; gusty wind bellows loudly. When the powerful wind stops, all these openings become totally silent. Don't you see how the branches and leaves still sway as the wind dies down?"

Ziyou said, "The music of earth comes from all the openings in the wilderness; the music of people is from flutes and musical instruments. What about the music of heaven?"

Ziqi replied, "All these thousands of different sounds are produced by the different shapes of the holes that the wind blows through. What made them that way? What do you suppose is the activating force behind it all?"

The Tao

道

The story ends on this note, because Master Ziqi deliberately refrains from describing the music of heaven explicitly, so the disciple can figure it out for himself.

By describing the music of earth, Master Ziqi shows that the wilderness, or nature itself, is in fact a musical instrument. When the wind blows through it, it is as if a human being is playing a flute. The underlying, unifying idea is that music is made when force moves through myriad openings. This is true when the breath of the flutist moves through the holes in the flute; it is just as true when the wind blows across the gaps in the wilderness.

When we take this metaphor another level higher, suddenly we can see that the entire universe is a musical instrument too. At this scale, we see that there is an omnipresent force that moves through everything in existence, including all living things and every human being.

Unlike the breath or the wind, this force is not a movement of air. It is a cosmic wind representing the living, dynamic power of creation and evolution. This is the activating force behind it all, and as it moves through all of us and everything around us, it creates beautiful music, a virtuoso symphony of awesome scope.

This music of heaven is not sound as we understand it. In it we can find rhythm, melody, harmony, and other aspects typical of music, but it cannot be heard. This music finds expression in the beauty of nature, the birth and death of stars and galaxies, and the simple dignity of human ideals.

You and I are part of the universal orchestra that produces this music of heaven. We are musicians as well as instruments. When the essence of the Tao flows through us, soundless tones emerge to form a transcendent song. This song is the purest expression of the soul.

天下萬物生於有，有生於無。

PART TWO

At Work

工作

One of the most common misconceptions is that Tao sages live in isolated hermitages. Those who believe this may find the Tao attractive because it represents an escape from civilization. They may be surprised to learn that true sages embrace all aspects of life—cities as well as the countryside, the office as well as the woods.

Many people think of work as drudgery—something to tolerate in order to make a living—but real Tao cultivators think of work as a great opportunity to cultivate. There are countless lessons to be learned in a typical working day. Once the eyes learn to observe the Tao, they see the Tao everywhere—in boardroom meetings, around the water cooler, in interactions with co-workers, and so on.

The teachings of the Tao apply very well to the corporate world. The Tao is the perfect tool to use when we encounter the following:

- *Adversities and setbacks*
- *The rollercoaster ride of a volatile market*
- *The critical boss, co-worker, or customer*

Tao cultivation also gives us essential skills to help us succeed. These skills include the following:

- *Channeling resentment into something more constructive*
- *Taking solid steps, one after another, toward our goal*
- *Forgiving those who, intentionally or unintentionally, have caused us damage*
- *Being objective, impartial, and able to see another point of view*
- *Remaining flexible in the face of constant change*
- *Listening to others with the Chi—spiritual energy—to achieve a higher level of understanding*

Chapter 7

The Donkey

What Can We Do When Bad Things Happen to Us?

井中之驢

Once upon a time in ancient China, the people at a village received orders from the regional governor to build a shrine for the emperor. If they could meet the deadline, the governor would reward them handsomely.

The chosen location for the shrine had a well, so they needed to fill it up before construction could take place. They brought in a donkey to transport piles of sand and mud for that purpose.

An accident occurred. The donkey got too close to the exposed well, lost his footing, and fell into it. The villagers tried to lift him out but could not. After many failed attempts, they realized it would take too long to rescue him.

Keeping the deadline in mind, the villagers decided to sacrifice the donkey. They proceeded to shovel the sand and mud into the well, thinking they had no choice but to bury him alive.

When the donkey realized what they were doing, he began to wail pitifully. The villagers heard him but ignored him. The value of the donkey wasn't much compared to the rewards they would get, so they continued to shovel.

After a while, the wailing stopped. The villagers wondered about this. Was the donkey dead already? Or did he just give up? What was going on?

Curious, they looked in the well. A surprising sight greeted them: The donkey was alive and well. When the mud and sand rained down on him, he shrugged them off, and then stamped around until they were tightly packed below him. This formed solid ground that lifted him a bit higher each time.

Eventually, the donkey got high enough inside the well. With one powerful leap, he jumped out of it. Amazed, the villagers watched as he trotted off with his head held high.

The Tao
道

Aren't you and I just like the donkey in the well sometimes? We all have days when we feel as if we are trapped. We can't get out, and there seems to be a never-ending stream of sand and mud raining down on us.

When we encounter adversity, our first impulse may be to complain. We ask ourselves questions like "Why does stuff like this always happen to me?" or "What have I done to deserve this?"

Just like the wailing of the donkey, our grievances have no effect whatsoever. The sand and mud continue to fall. Expressing outrage and feeling sorry for ourselves do not change anything.

In the story, the donkey came to the realization that his wailing was futile. In real life, many of us are not quite as intelligent. Even though we know it won't do any good, we still cry over spilled milk and wallow in bitterness.

This can become a repeating pattern of frustration followed by complaints followed by more frustration and more complaints. When we fall into this pattern, we cannot be at our best. The cycle of negativity prevents our mental state from being resourceful.

One way to break out of this pattern is to realize that we ourselves had a hand in authoring our fate—the good as well as the bad. Notice how the donkey was the one who carried the sand and mud next to the well. Whether he realized it or not, there was a note of irony in that he initiated the problem he complained about later.

I know a friend who could not stop talking about how miserable his life had become. He worked at a large corporation and was under constant pressure to perform. He had many co-workers and he did not get along with some of them. "I'm trapped," he said miserably. "I need to get out, but I can't."

He had all but forgotten that years ago he was the one who applied for an opening at this corporation. His goal was to work for a large organization, so he competed against other candidates aggressively, fought hard for the position, and won. Therefore, he was at the very least partially responsible for his subsequent misery.

Therefore, the question we really should ask isn't "What have I done to deserve this?" Rather, it is "What have I done to cause this?"

Once we break out of the complaining mode, we must then come to the realization that there is value in everything—even things we normally consider "bad." No matter what happens, there is always something we can learn from it. There is always some way for us to turn it from something negative to something positive.

Next, we deal with the adversity itself. We need to be able to shrug it off just as the donkey shrugged mud and sand off his body. To shrug it off doesn't mean pretending it never occurred. We recognize and acknowledge the event—with the crucial distinction that *we do not see it as a personal affront.*

The villagers continued to shovel mud and sand for their own reasons, not because they hated the donkey. Similarly, when something bad happens to us, it isn't because the universe has something against us. It is not an attack and it is not personal.

We then make use of negativity. The donkey used the mud and sand as building blocks. In the same way, we can use a negative event as the raw material to increase or enhance our spiritual cultivation. Some examples are as follows:

- *Has someone leveled a harsh criticism against us? That criticism may or may not contain a kernel of truth. If so, it shows us how we can improve. If not, it is a baseless attack that becomes a way for us to practice detachment from opinions that are not constructive.*

- *Has someone gotten in the way and blocked our path? It's an opportunity for us to reinforce our determination, strengthen our resolve, and increase our flexibility as we figure out a way around the obstacle.*
- *Has someone abandoned us or gone back on a promise? This is something we can use as a lesson that teaches us to become more independent and self-sufficient. Ultimately, we can only rely on ourselves.*
- *Has someone spread vicious and untrue rumors about us? If so, it's a reminder that we can live in such a way so that no one would ever believe them. It's also something that reveals the true nature of the people around us—a convenient way to find out who our real friends are.*

When we look at it from this perspective, we quickly realize that there isn't anything we cannot use in some way. We can even say that everything that happens can be "good" because we can make it serve us in some capacity. No matter what kind of sand or mud is falling on us, we can step on it and use it to elevate ourselves a little higher.

The more we do this, the better we get at it. Each negative event that occurs becomes just another helpful stepping-stone. Every adversity moves us up, until we rise to the level of the Tao sages, who are known for their ability to handle anything with calmness and composure. Now we begin to understand their secret!

Just like the donkey jumping out of the well, we will be able to transcend beyond the mud and sand. Negativity and adversity no longer have any power over us and may as well not exist. The prison of bitter complaints disappears below us as we make the leap.

We are no longer trapped in the well!

勝人者有力，自勝者強。

Chapter 8

Misfortunes and Blessings

Gracefully Dealing with the Ups and Downs of Life

禍與福

In the northern frontier of ancient China, there lived a man who was particularly skilled in raising horses. People knew of him and called him Sai Ong—literally "Old Frontiersman."

One day, for some unknown reason, his horse got loose and ran off into the Hu territory beyond the Great Wall. The Hu tribes were hostile toward the Chinese, so everyone assumed the horse was as good as lost.

Horses were very valuable to the people living at the frontier, so they regarded this loss as a great financial setback. They visited Sai Ong to express their sympathies, but Sai Ong's elderly father surprised them by remaining calm and unaffected.

Much to their puzzlement, the old man asked: "Who says this cannot be some sort of blessing?"

Months later, the horse returned to the stable with a companion—a fine steed of the Hu breed. It was as if Sai Ong's wealth suddenly doubled. Everyone came by to marvel at the new horse and to congratulate him, but again his elderly father showed no great emotions. He said: "Who says this cannot be some sort of misfortune?"

Sai Ong's son enjoyed riding and took the new horse out for a ride. An accident occurred, causing him to fall badly and break a leg. Again sympathetic people came to console the family, and again they saw that the grandfather remained as calm as ever. Just as before, he told them: "Who says this cannot be some sort of blessing?"

One year later, the Hu people amassed and crossed the border into China. All the able-bodied young men were summoned into the army to take up arms in defense. Fierce battles ensued, resulting in heavy casualties. Among the inhabitants of the northern frontier, nine out of ten men died.

Sai Ong's son did not go into battle because of his broken leg. As a result, he was spared that terrible fate, and his family survived the war intact.

Thus, blessings may turn out to be misfortunes, and misfortunes blessings. They change from one to the other endlessly; the workings of destiny have a truly fathomless depth.

The Tao

道

The above is faithful rendition of the Chinese story, taken directly from the ancient *Huainanzi* text. It is one of the classics that form the fabric of Chinese culture. The Chinese people know the story well, and have coined a phrase to summarize it: "Sai Ong loses horse. Who knows if it isn't a blessing?"

The phrase is especially applicable when you encounter a situation that seems completely against you. When you feel frustrated, discouraged, or hopeless, this phrase reminds you that things may not be as they first appear.

The sages teach that everything happens for a reason. Temporary defeats and disappointments all contain the golden kernel of a lesson custom-made for you. Just as you must lower yourself in order to jump higher, learning the lesson in a spirit of humility will give you the extra energy you need to fly over the next hurdle. And when you look at it this way, who says that the negative stuff cannot be some sort of good news in disguise?

The Tao is all about balance, so the other side of the teaching is just as valid and valuable. We can see how we need not dwell on depression and discouragement to the point where they rob us of the ability to act. The flip side of the coin is just as true. That is, when we encounter something that appears to be an advantage, we need not let ourselves get carried away with ecstatic excitement so that we become blind to the seed of adversity hiding inside the advancement.

Every dark cloud has a silver lining—conversely, the silver lining frames a dark cloud. Or as chapter 58 of *Tao Te Ching* expresses it:

Misfortune is what fortune depends upon
Fortune is where misfortune hides beneath

Yin contains yang; yang contains yin. Every failure harbors the hidden seed of future success; every triumph contains the covert cause of future defeat. Thus, Sai Ong's father isn't mortified by bad news—but neither is he overelated by what others consider good news.

It all comes down to the path of moderation. Without moderation, life is like a roller coaster ride. It may be thrilling at first, but the nonstop peaks and valleys soon wear you out and make it impossible for you to have peace of mind. One moment you are high on victory; the next you crash and burn.

With moderation, life gets closer to the graceful and effortless *wu wei* ideal, the ideal of actions without attachments. You still experience joy and sorrow, but not the debilitating intensities of extreme emotions. You partake fully in both celebration and grieving, but never overdo either one to excess. Instead of nonstop peaks and valleys, life becomes a series of gentle rolling hills. The extreme ups and downs become the exceptions, not the rule.

This does not mean we become wooden or devoid of strong emotions. Nor does it mean that life becomes *diluted* in some way. The lesson does not teach bland acceptance of whatever life offers, nor is it an excuse to avoid taking action.

What it *does* mean is that we no longer cling to emotions. The practice of emotional detachment allows us to observe life much more clearly, so that when blessing turns to misfortune or vice versa, it does not take us by surprise. We are ready to react with clarity, and we recognize the transformation as part of the complex workings of the Tao—nothing more and nothing less.

Ultimately, this story teaches us that *things simply happen in life*. They are not good or bad—they just are. They all serve the greater purpose of providing life lessons, but if we are too quick to judge them as good or bad based on initial impressions, we run the risk of losing sight of the real lessons.

So next time something "bad" happens to you and makes you feel upset, remember: *Sai Ong loses horse. Who knows if it isn't a blessing?*

禍兮，福之所倚；福兮，禍之所伏。

Chapter 9
The Wolves

What Is the Best Way to Handle Negative People?

心中之狼

"*Master, you must help me,*" *said the visitor.* "*I am at my wit's end.*"

"*What seems to be the problem?*" *the sage asked.*

"*I am having a hard time controlling my anger,*" *the visitor said.* "*It's just the way people are. I see them criticizing others while totally unaware of their own faults. I do not wish to criticize them because I don't want to be like them, but it really upsets me.*"

"*I see,*" *said the sage.* "*Tell me something first: Aren't you the villager who narrowly escaped death last year?*"

"*Yes,*" *the visitor nodded.* "*It was a terrible experience. I ventured too far into the forest and ran into a pack of hungry wolves.*"

"What did you do?"

"I climbed up a tree just in time before they converged on me. These wolves were big and I had no doubt they could tear me to pieces."

"So you were trapped?"

"Yes. I knew I wouldn't last long without water and food, so I waited for them to relax their guard. When I thought it was safe enough, I would jump down, make a mad dash for the next tree, and then climb up before they converged again."

"This sounds like quite an ordeal."

"Yes—altogether it lasted two days. I thought I would surely die. Luckily a group of hunters approached when I got close enough to the village. The wolves scattered and I was saved."

"I'm curious about one thing," said the sage. "During the experience, were you ever offended by the wolves?"

"What? Offended?"

"Yes. Did you feel offended, or insulted by the wolves?"

"Of course not, Master. That thought never crossed my mind."

"Why not? They wanted nothing more than to bite into you, did they not? They wanted to kill you, did they not?"

"Yes, but that is what wolves do! They were just being themselves. It would be absurd for me to take offense."

The Tao

道

Criticizing others while being unaware of their own faults is something that many people do. We can even say that it is something we all do from time to time. In a sense, the ravenous wolves live in every one of us.

If we are deep in the woods and encounter wolves who close in on us, we should not just stand there. We should certainly protect ourselves by getting away if at all possible. Similarly, when people lash out at us with venomous criticism, we should not accept it passively. We should certainly protect ourselves by putting some distance between us and them if at all possible; protect ourselves in other ways if not.

The crucial point is that we can do so without feeling offended or insulted, because these people are simply being themselves. It is their nature to be critical and judgmental, so it would be absurd for us to take offense. It would be pointless to get angry.

Next time these hungry wolves in human skin converge, remember: it's just the way people are—exactly as the visitor said when he first came in.

知人者智，自知者明。

Chapter 10
The Soft Overcomes the Hard

Directing Energy into Building Internal Strength

以柔克剛

One day, a young man visited with the sage and complained bitterly about his job at the local store.

"The boss has no respect for my talents," he told the sage. "He does not give me the authority I deserve and ignores the sensible ideas I suggest. I've had all I can take of this rudeness. I am going to march into his office, give him a piece of my mind, and quit!"

The sage asked: "How much do you know about the business of the store? Do you know how they keep track of profits, expenses, or inventory?"

"Not really. Why do you ask?"

"If you resign right now, they won't see it as a big loss because you don't possess any valuable knowledge. A much better plan to have your revenge is to learn everything about their business before you quit. Take advantage of them by using the store as a free source of training. When you leave, your departure will come as a crushing blow, and you'll walk away with all their business secrets."

"That's a great idea," the young man said. "It'll really make them regret looking down on me. I'll show them!"

He put the plan into action. He used stolen moments throughout the day to covertly learn the many aspects of the business. He cut short his breaks and stayed after hours in order to spend more time perfecting his newly acquired knowledge.

A year later, the sage ran into him at the market and greeted him. "How goes your plan for revenge? Have you learned enough to quit?"

"Yes, I have, but . . . the boss has changed completely! He values my work and frequently compliments me. In the past few months he gave me important assignments, a promotion, and a raise! Everything is different now, and . . . well, I don't really want to quit!"

The Tao

道

It was exactly as the sage expected. The sage knew that when the young man failed to gain respect initially, it might not be because of rudeness, but simply because of his lack of abilities and his failure to apply himself. The young man could not see his own faults. He felt he was right and entitled to more praise than he received.

Tao Te Ching, chapter 24, describes this mindset as follows:

Those who presume themselves are not distinguished
Those who praise themselves have no merit

Lao Tzu's message is clear: Those who presume, or think they are always right, will not be considered respectable or admirable by others; those who incessantly praise themselves do not possess true merit. This is why the young man did not gain the recognition to which he felt entitled.

To what extent do these lines also describe you and me? We may assume that we are far wiser than the young man, but surveys consistently reveal that most people feel contempt for their managers. The truth is, we often complain about the boss or the management, and many of us contemplate quitting from time to time.

In our conflict-oriented culture, we have a tendency to counter force with force. If someone yells at us, we yell back louder. When we feel disrespected, our first impulse is to give that disrespect right back—just like the young man. Some of us even take pride in this and openly proclaim that we give as good as we get.

Thus, the conventional approach is all about confrontation and clashing. It is the "hard" path to traverse through life because it focuses on the external manifestations of power. Its method is to pump up the self by diminishing others.

The Tao approach isn't about confrontation and clashing. Instead, it is all about redirecting and channeling. It is the "soft" path because it focuses on internal strength. Its goal is to improve oneself so that everyone can win.

When the young man spoke of his initial plan to quit, his primary thought was that it would be the quickest way to vent his frustration. He could feel better by hurling back the rudeness he perceived. By diminishing others in this manner, he would gain a satisfying victory.

Or would he? After the venting and quitting, he would be out of a job. He would be financially worse off and no wiser than before. The victory that he thought would be satisfying would quickly become shallow and meaningless. His conventional approach would yield a conventional result: a life with more discord and strife.

The sage saw this and nudged him into a completely different direction. The energy most people devote to lashing out and damaging others is considerable. The sage redirected and channeled this energy into a constructive path—a path that led to a real, meaningful, and lasting victory.

At this point we may find ourselves wondering: "But what if the boss is really horrible so that no matter how hard you try, nothing you do is ever good enough? Then wouldn't you be wasting time and effort learning about the business?"

Not at all. Bad bosses and poor managers certainly exist, but the sage's teaching remains true. When the young man became truly distinguished and accumulated real merits through disciplined effort, he would receive recognition and respect no matter what—if not from his own boss, then certainly from the store's competitors. His result would remain the same: a real, meaningful, and lasting victory.

This teaching isn't new. Lao Tzu wrote repeatedly that the soft overcomes the hard. Jesus taught us to turn the other cheek. We even have a common saying that living well (as opposed to striking back) is the best revenge. These are all profound wisdom and echoes of the Tao approach. But despite our familiarity with the concept, it is not something most of us can apply to daily life.

It is exactly as *Tao Te Ching*, chapter 78, points out:

That the weak overcomes the strong
And the soft overcomes the hard
Everybody in the world knows
But cannot put into practice

It may be because the Tao approach is inwardly directed and lacks conspicuous external manifestations (animosity, arguments, fights). This can easily give people the misleading impression of weakness and cowardice, when in reality the Tao approach requires uncommon courage and willpower.

When we encounter injuries of any kind, our instinctive response is one of hatred as well as a powerful desire to get even. We want an eye for an eye. We wish to repay in kind or fight fire with fire. There is definitely a part of us that is contentious in nature.

Few people have the spiritual strength and understanding to transcend this contentiousness. It is not an easy lesson to master, but at least the *Tao Te Ching* highlights the difficulty so we can pay special attention to this aspect of cultivation. It also gives us a useful analogy by comparing the Tao approach to water. Water is seemingly soft and weak, and yet has the tremendous power to penetrate, dissolve, and wash away rocks. Keeping this analogy in mind makes it easier for us to apply the principle in everyday situations.

When we master this lesson, the results can be dramatic. The young man said his boss changed and everything was different. In reality, it was he who changed, and that alone made all the difference in the world.

That is exactly the way it can work for us as well. When you make a gut-level decision to commit yourself to this teaching, to be like water and allow the soft to overcome the hard . . . that is when your world, your life, and your fate will undergo a startling transformation. When you improve your character and elevate your spiritual understanding by utilizing the Tao approach . . . that is when your destiny will never be the same again!

弱之勝強，柔之勝剛。

Chapter 11
The Third Floor

Achieving Real and Lasting Results

腳踏實地

One day, a wealthy man went to another village for a visit. There he saw an imposing mansion that stood three stories tall. He found it most impressive and complimented the owner on this great achievement. The owner thanked him and invited him in for a tour. Together they went up to the third floor, where they took in a commanding view of the countryside.

After the wealthy man returned to his own village, he decided he wanted the same thing. He summoned a master mason and described what he had in mind. The mason said: "You're talking to the right person—I'm the one who built that mansion!"

The wealthy man was pleased: "Great! Then you know exactly what I want. Please get started as soon as possible."

The mason assembled a crew and began building. The wealthy man had never seen a construction before, so he visited the site to take a look. What he saw there baffled him, so he asked the mason: "What is the crew doing?"

"Oh, they're working on the foundation."

"Why?"

The mason did not think the wealthy man was serious, but decided to humor him since he was footing the bill: "Because we build the first floor on top of the foundation—of course."

"But why do you need the first floor?"

Now the mason was certain the wealthy man was joking, so he played along: "Well, we want to build the second floor on top of the first floor."

"And you need the second floor for . . . what exactly?"

The mason was confused, because he could tell the wealthy man was completely serious. Not knowing what else to say, he replied: "Sir, obviously we'll put the third floor on top of the second floor."

"No! Stop!" the wealthy man exclaimed. "This is a big mistake. I'm glad I'm here to clear it up. I only want the third floor. You don't need to build the foundation and the first two floors. That ought to save us a lot of time and money!"

The Tao
道

Doesn't this story seem ludicrous? Isn't it easy to understand that we must start at the bottom and work our way up? How can anyone expect to have the third floor without the floors below it?

But if it is really that easy to understand, why are get-rich-quick schemes still so popular? Can it be because we want to be wealthy (the third floor) but we don't want to work industriously (the foundation), save money (the first floor), and invest wisely (the second floor)?

How did diet pills become a $17 billion industry? Can it be because we want to be thinner (the third floor) but we don't want to eat less (the foundation), exercise more (the first floor), and sustain this discipline over a long period of time (the second floor)?

Lao Tzu addresses this in *Tao Te Ching,* chapter 70:

My words are easy to understand, easy to practice
The world cannot understand, cannot practice

It is easy for us to understand that in order to achieve something, we must build the framework and create the necessary conditions. But something is lost when we go from concept to reality; our intellectual understanding does not translate to the real world. We still want something for nothing, even though we know that if it sounds too good to be true, it probably is. We still want shortcuts.

This is also something noted by Lao Tzu, in chapter 53 of *Tao Te Ching:*

The great Tao is broad and plain
But people like the side paths

It is not difficult to traverse the great Tao—it is a wide and flat road, perfect for travelers. We walk this road one step at a time. It is the essence of simplicity. What can possibly be simpler?

But simplicity doesn't seem to be what most people want. Rather than taking the certain path slowly but surely, people are enticed by the bright, colorful, flashing signs by the side of the road. These signs say things like "No Previous Experience Necessary" or "Lose Weight While You Sleep" or "Powerful New Technology! Results Guaranteed!"

We all know the saying that the great thousand-mile journey starts with one step. We've all heard it many times, and it is indeed a timeless truth. But there is another part to it that is equally important: that first step is followed by another step, then another, and another, and so on until the great journey is completed.

In fact, it takes about two thousand steps to walk a mile, so a thousand-mile journey would equal roughly two million steps. In order to have any hope of completing the journey, the traveler must be completely committed to taking every single one of those steps.

This realization may seem odd. When we talk about the great journey as a combination of so many steps, doesn't it seem difficult and tedious? In Asian traditions, the freedom of the Tao has always walked hand in hand with long-term, sustained discipline. The two are flip sides of the same coin.

The key realization is that diligent work doesn't have to be tedious. When you make it part of your life pattern, disciplined effort becomes natural. And when you engage in this natural part of your life, you discover in it an effortless ease and carefree joy all its own.

This is really the best way to cultivate. It is a down-to-earth and practical approach that emphasizes consistent action—the simple action of putting one foot in front of the other in the great journey. This is our discipline.

The Chinese would say this is cultivation with "feet stepping on solid ground." The side paths, with their endless promises of a third floor floating in midair, are nothing but illusions. The only real, solid ground we have is the broad and plain path of the Tao. You and I have already taken our first steps on it. Let us continue walking together on this great Tao . . . one solid step after another!

大道甚夷，而民好徑。

Chapter 12

The Tao of Forgiveness

How Do We Forgive Those Who Have Offended Us?

真正的原諒

One day, the sage gave the disciple an empty sack and a basket of potatoes. "Think of all the people who have done or said something against you in the recent past, especially those you cannot forgive. For each of them, inscribe the name on a potato and put it in the sack."

The disciple came up with quite a few names, and soon his sack was heavy with potatoes.

"Carry the sack with you wherever you go for a week," said the sage. "We'll talk after that."

At first, the disciple thought nothing of it. Carrying the sack was not particu-

larly difficult. But after a while, it became more of a burden. It sometimes got in the way, and it seemed to require more effort to carry as time went on, even though its weight remained the same.

After a few days, the sack began to stink. The carved potatoes gave off a ripe odor. Not only were they increasingly inconvenient to carry around, they were also becoming rather unpleasant.

Finally, the week was over. The sage summoned the disciple. "Any thoughts about all this?"

"Yes, Master," the disciple replied. "When we are unable to forgive others, we carry negative feelings with us everywhere, much like these potatoes. That negativity becomes a burden to us and, after a while, it festers."

"Yes, that is exactly what happens when one holds a grudge. So, how can we lighten the load?"

"We must strive to forgive."

"Forgiving someone is the equivalent of removing the corresponding potato from the sack. How many of your transgressors are you able to forgive?"

"I've thought about it quite a bit, Master," the disciple said. "It required much effort, but I have decided to forgive all of them."

"Very well, we can remove all the potatoes. Were there any more people who transgressed against you this last week?"

The disciple thought for a while and admitted there were. Then he felt panic when he realized his empty sack was about to get filled up again.

"Master," he asked, "if we continue like this, wouldn't there always be potatoes in the sack week after week?"

"Yes, as long as people speak or act against you in some way, you will always have potatoes."

"But Master, we can never control what others do. So what good is the Tao in this case?"

"We're not at the realm of the Tao yet. Everything we have talked about so far is the conventional approach to forgiveness. It is the same thing that many philosophies and most religions preach—we must constantly strive to forgive, for it is an important virtue. This is not the Tao because there is no striving in the Tao."

"Then what is the Tao, Master?"

"You can figure it out. If the potatoes are negative feelings, then what is the sack?"

"The sack is . . . that which allows me to hold on to the negativity. It is something within us that makes us dwell on feeling offended. . . . Ah, it is my inflated sense of self-importance."

"And what will happen if you let go of it?"

"Then . . . the things that people do or say against me no longer seem like such a major issue."

"In that case, you won't have any names to inscribe on potatoes. That means no more weight to carry around, and no more bad smells. The Tao of forgiveness is the conscious decision not just to remove some potatoes, but to relinquish the entire sack."

The Tao

道

The conventional approach to forgiveness, as the sage points out, is focused on striving. There is a poem by Shenxiu, the Zen monk, that describes this precisely:

Body is the bodhi tree
Heart is like clear mirror stand
Strive to clean it constantly
Do not let the dust motes land

It is all about constant, diligent practice. The process never stops, because there will always be more dust falling on the clear mirror. Just when you think you've got it perfectly clean, another speck of dust has landed. The disciple noted that as long as he remained at this level, his sack would never run out of potatoes. Similarly, as long as we're stuck in the conventional approach to forgiveness, we'll never run out of transgressors to forgive.

But why is there a mirror for the dust to fall on in the first place? And does it really need to be there?

The mirror in the poem can represent egoism—an exaggerated sense of conceit and vanity. Although it does not exist as a physical thing, we treat it as such. Our language is full of references to this assumption. We talk about the "bruised" ego, or how the pride is "hurt," or how one's dignity can be "wounded"—as if egoism were part of the body, like a limb or an organ.

And yet egoism is nothing more than a construction of the mind. It springs from the false perception that we are separate and different from others. That sense of separation and difference leads us to skewed comparisons, which in turn lead us to a false conviction of superiority. When this elaborate illusion is under attack, the illusory injuries seem quite real. But as soon as we see through the illusion, it fades away, and so do the damages against it.

This is the basis of the Tao approach to forgiveness. Zen Master Huineng's response to Shenxiu's poem illustrates it perfectly:

Bodhi really has no tree
Nor is clear mirror the stand
Nothing's there initially
So where can the dust motes land?

The mirror doesn't really exist. Although the dust motes keep falling, there is nothing for them to land on or cling to, and there is nothing to wipe clean. Egoism is something we created for ourselves, so it is something we can dismiss with a simple decision. Without egoism there is nothing to bruise, hurt, or wound. Without damages or injuries to the ego, pride, or dignity, there is also nothing to forgive.

This is how the sage transcends beyond the ordinary teachings of forgiveness. By recognizing that the true self can never be hurt, and it is only the false projections of the ego that are damaged by criticisms and insults, we bypass the constant striving to forgive others.

Not many people realize this particular realm of the Tao even exists, but once we have truly arrived—absorbed the lesson completely—forgiveness for us will require no effort at all. Forgiving becomes an obsolete and unnecessary action, as this Tao takes us through life with smooth, effortless ease and elegance.

菩提本無樹，明鏡亦非臺，本來無一物，何處惹塵埃。

Chapter 13

The Shields

Seeing Both Sides of an Issue

一體兩面

A warrior was out for a stroll one sunny day. As he made his way through the woods, he saw another warrior also taking a walk. They greeted each other in friendly fashion.

Then, a glint of reflected light caught their eyes. They saw two shields lying on the ground not far away. One was silver and the other was gold. Even from a distance they could tell that the shields were of extremely high quality.

"What a find!" the first warrior exclaimed. "I shall take the golden shield. You can have the silver." He started toward them.

"Not so, my friend. I saw them first. The golden shield belongs to me. I can grant

you the silver shield." The second warrior walked faster toward the shields, and the first warrior picked up speed to match.

"Thank you for your generosity, but it is not necessary. I voiced my claim before you did, thus the golden shield is mine by right. You should be glad I am willing to let you have the silver." They both began jogging.

"Your claim does not matter, for I outrank you. Therefore it shall be as I command: gold for me, silver for you." It became a race. Both men ran full-tilt toward the shields.

"Your rank means nothing, for we serve different lords. These woods belong to my lord. I shall retrieve the golden shield for him; the silver shield is a fitting tribute for your lord." It was becoming apparent that they were well matched in speed. Neither would get to the shields before the other.

"These woods belong to no one. I am the superior swordsman and I say the golden shield is mine. If you wish to contest my claim, you must face my sword." The warrior drew his weapon, and his opponent did likewise.

A fierce battle ensued. The two warriors discovered that they were also well matched in swordsmanship. Neither could gain the upper hand over the other. It became a contest of endurance—the first to tire and falter would lose the fight, and thus the golden shield.

Unfortunately, the two warriors were also well matched in stamina. After fighting for more than an hour, both became equally exhausted. Still they persisted, until neither one could remain standing any longer. Each collapsed to the ground at the same time, panting and gasping for breath, but still eyeing the other warily.

They looked at the cause of their conflict. From this lower perspective, they could see the shields edgewise. The golden shield looked like it had a silver side underneath, and the silver shield . . .

"Are you thinking what I'm thinking?" one warrior asked the other.

"We should take a closer look."

"No tricks."

"Agreed."

In unison, each warrior reached out with his sword to flip a shield over. It was as they suspected: the two shields were identical gold on one side and silver on the other!

The Tao

道

The only way we can approach the Tao is to relax the death grip of logic, and engage the far more powerful tool of intuition. When the rationality of the brain utterly fails to grasp the Tao, the heart will step in to embrace it with a way of knowing that is beyond knowledge. Feeling is the key.

The warriors came to the realization that their battle was meaningless. All along, the shields were the same, and each of them could take one and be perfectly satisfied. All that effort and strife, all the verbal jousting and physical combat, was for nothing.

Aren't we just like the warriors sometimes? We struggle against other people, trying to get ahead or gain an advantage, but for what? When we are exhausted and stressed out by all the contention, conflict, and competition, will we also find that the objective we strive for is completely meaningless?

Another lesson from this tale is that hostility and ill will often come about when we can see only one side of an issue. Discord rears its ugly head when both sides of a dispute are totally convinced of their own righteousness. Each side stubbornly clings to its own perspective while refusing to—or perhaps being unable to—see the other side.

What would happen if we could see more than just our side? By being able to perceive how others look at the same thing, we can understand how the conflict began in the first place. This better understanding leads to a better solution—most likely one that does not require contention or violence! And that, in turn, leads to greater peace and harmony.

This is why Tao cultivators always seek more than one perspective. They know that when they can view something from many different angles, they gain greater understanding and wisdom. Then, just like the warriors, they will come to the realization that struggles and strife are the opposite of the Tao—and completely unnecessary!

萬物負陰而抱陽，沖氣以為和。

Chapter 14

The Tao of Change

Facing the Changes in Life and Mastering Them

改變之道

While alive, the body is soft and pliant
When dead, it is hard and rigid
All living things, grass and trees,
While alive, are soft and supple
When dead, become dry and brittle
Thus that which is hard and stiff
Is the follower of death
That which is soft and pliant
Is the follower of life

The Tao

道

By linking the living with flexibility in chapter 76 of *Tao Te Ching*, Lao Tzu is emphasizing the adaptable nature of life and the importance of being flexible as the way to live, to thrive, and to succeed. The consequence of inflexibility is nothing less than death itself.

This concept fits well with the yin and yang symbol. At a higher level of understanding, we see that the symbol represents the endless motions of the cosmos, and not a static scene as it may seem at first. The line between yin and yang is a curve, suggesting fluidity and flow. Taken as a whole, the symbol depicts a reality that is dynamic, active, constantly revolving, and in essence alive.

The message is clear: the world never stops changing, and the only way to deal with change is to maintain flexibility. If we refuse to be flexible, we are in effect opting out of the game of life. The world moves on without us.

In this day and age, rapid changes overtake us and companies scramble to keep up. What Lao Tzu points out for individuals is just as valid for organizations: remain flexible and stay in business, or refuse to yield and become extinct. When a critical juncture comes and a company must regroup and retool to remain competitive, there will always be those who resist. You know who they are, because they are always the ones who say things like "Oh, that does not apply to us," or "Don't fix something that ain't broke," or "We should keep doing it this way because that's how we've always done it."

The ideas in this teaching are simple. Perhaps it is because of the simplicity that we tend to forget all about them in our day-to-day rat race. When we settle into a comfortable (or at least tolerable) situation, inertia sets in and it is very much human nature to become complacent. We slow down, stop learning and growing, and start losing whatever flexibility and dynamism we had before.

Is it possible for you to stagnate mentally, emotionally, financially, or spiritually, and not be aware that you are stuck in a rut or spinning your wheels? Of course it is. It happens all the time to the best of us, and that's why we need a reminder every now and then.

This very real, human need makes the simplicity of the message an important strength. When the timing is right, such a message can hit you like a ton of bricks. It wakes you up and forces you to confront the fact that you are no longer living life to the fullest. Simplicity, in this case, makes it that much more direct and powerful. "My goodness," you may say to yourself as you take stock of your situation, "why didn't I see this sooner?"

We often cannot see it clearly because our reasoning powers and emotional attachments refuse to let us. They spin a complex web of rationalization and self-delusion that obscure the truth. We can overcome this by expressing the Tao from a fresh perspective, so that an old teaching suddenly appears in a new light. This clarity lets us see that this Tao is ultimately about the eternal change and the way we choose to deal with it. We can call it the Tao of Change.

道常無為，而無不為。

Chapter 15

Xin Zhai

How to Understand What Is Really Going On

心齋

Yen Hui visited Confucius to bid farewell. He told his master that he was going to Wei, which was at the time a turbulent and dangerous land.

"Why do you want to go there?" Confucius wanted to know.

"I heard that the Wei King is quite a tyrant and his people are suffering, Master. He does not value human life and wages war carelessly. The countryside is filled with dead bodies. You've taught us to treat a chaotic nation as a doctor treats the wounded, so I feel I should make an attempt."

"Absurd!" Confucius exclaimed. "You don't even know what you're doing! How can you help other people? The second you open your mouth in front of this tyrant,

he will dominate you with his power and order your execution. Do you have a plan to avoid that?"

"Uh . . . how about a simple and direct approach?" asked Yen Hui.

"No," replied Confucius. "The Wei King is a willful man and not accustomed to being contradicted. His most likely reaction to your direct approach will be to bully you, and there won't be anything you can do about it."

"Very well. Instead of directly opposing him, I shall be clever and appear to yield. In order to steer him in the right direction, I will cite traditions and past examples instead of my own idea. This way, I can be perfectly honest and yet avoid offending him."

"Wrong again." The master still disapproved. "At best this plan will let you survive with your hide intact, but you simply won't be able to produce any significant changes in the land of Wei. The Wei King's overpowering ego will only be boosted by your passive approach; you will only make him even more convinced that he's right."

At this point Yen Hui was out of ideas. If one couldn't use the direct approach or the indirect approach, then surely the situation was completely hopeless? "What other approach is there, Master?"

Confucius said: "Xin Zhai is the way."

Yen Hui asked: "Xin Zhai? Would that be a direct or indirect approach?"

"Xin Zhai is not necessarily direct or indirect; it is beyond such trifling distinctions. You already know that the purpose of Zhai—vegetarian diet—is to cleanse your physiology. In the same way, the purpose of Xin Zhai is to cleanse your mind. Approach the Wei King with a cleansed mind, and you shall be able to achieve your purpose."

The Tao
道

The methods Yen Hui proposed, direct and indirect, were based on a host of preconceptions and assumptions. They were the product of logic and reasoning, and came replete with moves, countermoves, scenarios, and contingencies. Xin Zhai was at a level above this, with the mandate of being totally free of preconceptions or assumptions. This state, called "emptiness," leads to a state of oneness with any situation.

What Xin Zhai enables one to do is listen, not with the ear or the mind, but with the Chi. When you listen with your ears, you hear the propagation of sound waves through the air. When you listen with your mind, you decipher the sounds into words and receive the meaning the speaker intends to convey.

When you listen with the Chi, you begin to see through the hidden agendas, misdirections, and half-truths. This lets you glimpse the true reality and capture insights that would normally elude the ears and the mind.

This is why Confucius instructed Yen Hui to clear his mind with Xin Zhai. This would free him from any preoccupation with the self or preconceived limitations. Such an egoless approach would allow Yen Hui to act upon others without coming into conflict with their private conceits. By listening to the self-centered tyrant and understanding the reality behind his words, Yen Hui could gain the mental foothold he needed to work his influence.

We can use Confucius's idea for ourselves. For many issues in life, the usual thought-out, reasoned-out plans are quite adequate. When we are facing a challenge, however, such plans have an annoying tendency to suddenly become useless when events take an unforeseen turn.

This is a broad stroke that covers a lot of human endeavors, from grand enterprises to personal misadventures. For instance, you may go to an important job interview with a script in your mind. The script is full of intelligent responses and remarks you had crafted so you would know exactly what to say in any situation. But then the interviewer refuses to follow your great script and takes the conversation in a totally bizarre direction, and much to your exasperation, all the carefully crafted responses and remarks are out the window!

In a situation like that, you can see that Xin Zhai is definitely the superior approach. Don't bother thinking up clever lines or some contrived ways to look cool. Instead, free your mind of unnecessary obstructions like worries, apprehensions, and useless speculations on what other people may think about you. Once your ego and vanity are out of the way, you will be able to get into the interview with your entire being, without prejudgment.

Listening with Xin Zhai and following one's intuition will produce nearly miraculous results because most of us would love to have someone really listen to us, and yet we never listen to others in the same way. Hence the state of Xin Zhai makes one perfectly natural, appealing, and completely different from everyone else.

Next time you find yourself confronted by difficult people, take heart. Remember the lesson of Xin Zhai and know that you have a great tool that will help you. Collect yourself, let go of your ego, clear your preconceptions, and really listen. Follow your instincts and let your powerful subconscious mind guide you through the labyrinth of hidden agendas, misdirections, and half-truths. Once you have mastered this process, you will be amazed by the ease with which you can achieve rapport and agreement with others. Such is the power of Xin Zhai.

聖人無常心，以百姓心為心。

PART THREE

With Friends

朋友

Our friends reflect who we are inside. This truth holds so well that we can even use it as a gauge of our level of cultivation. Do they inspire us? Are they worthy of admiration? If so, chances are excellent that we are also on the right track.

The Tao of interpersonal relationship is at work whenever we get together with our friends. The more we understand this Tao, the more our social interactions tend to be full of harmony, positive energy, and fun.

In cultivating this aspect of life, there are some important things we must do:

- *Focus on character—the inner attributes of our friends.*
- *Let go of the obsessive need to compare against one another.*
- *Become involved in the community.*
- *Get to know what is inside someone's heart.*
- *Initiate the karmic cycle of giving and receiving abundantly.*
- *Understand the power of flattery and be able to recognize it.*
- *Manage the ego.*

Chapter 16

Feeding the Clothes

Looking Deeper Than the Superficial

以貌取人

One day, the sage received an invitation from a friend. They hadn't seen each other for quite some time, so the friend wanted to invite the sage over for dinner.

The sage went to the address indicated and saw that it was a grand mansion. Apparently his friend had done quite well recently.

The doorman stopped the sage. Because the sage dressed plainly, the doorman assumed he must be a solicitor and turned him away.

Amused by this, the sage changed into his ceremonial robe and went to the mansion again. The doorman still failed to recognize him, but assumed he must be someone important. The sage was led inside the mansion, where he found his friend waiting.

When dinner began, the sage ate none of the food but kept stuffing appetizers and dumplings into his pockets. His host found this most puzzling, and said: "Master, you don't need to do that. We can prepare a bag for you to take home later on. Please relax and enjoy the meal."

The sage told him: "When I came here earlier wearing plain clothes, I was blocked at the front door. After I changed into this robe, I was welcomed inside. Obviously you invited my robe instead of me, so it is only reasonable that the robe should enjoy your food!"

The Tao

道

One of the most appealing things about the study of the Tao is the sense of humor that permeates it. Although far from frivolous, sages never take themselves too seriously. Thus, something that another person might interpret as a dreadful insult (such as being refused entrance) to a sage would be simply an interesting opportunity to observe human nature at work.

Sages may also use humor to convey the points they wish to make. They have found this to be far more effective and readily accepted than stern lectures. As the Taoist philosopher Chuang Tzu demonstrated with his many tales, laughter that lightens the heart and brightens the day can take us further down the path of cultivation.

The aspect of human nature that the sage observed in the story was superficiality. We have a tendency to judge others based on external appearance. Just as the doorman failed to recognize the sage, we often fail to recognize the real individuals around us in everyday life.

The sage did not rail against this or complain about it. He knew this was how most people operated. If he were to struggle against human nature and try to change others, it would simply be an exercise in futility.

The sage was quite willing to dress appropriately for the given setting. As a general rule, Tao cultivators do not flaunt their unconventional outlook on life, and therefore do not dress to shock, stand out, or attract attention. They have no need to prove how "cool" they are by rebelling against conventions.

Tao cultivators also aren't people who look unkempt and justify it by claiming to follow their inner nature. A real cultivator would recognize this as intellectual sophistry covering up a lack of discipline. Being presentable demonstrates respect to people with whom we interact. It is a courtesy we extend to others.

In the story, the sage pointed out in his unique way how ludicrous it is for us to judge a book by its cover. We all know that external appearance is transient while the inner essence remains constant. And yet we focus so much on the external, we have begun to treat the transient as if it were real. Not only are we judging a book by its cover, we are ignoring all the pages in the book and regarding the cover as the book.

Consider the celebrity culture of our modern times. Consider how we often idolize actors and models based on external appearance. We are impressed by them primarily because of their physical beauty. This is not so different from the doorman deferring to the sage when he showed up in his ceremonial robe.

Never before in history has external appearance been so highly valued. In ancient China, teachers and scholars were far more highly regarded than performers. Today we have the exact opposite. As a society, we heap praise and financial rewards upon celebrities. This is not so different from the sage stuffing food into the pockets of his robe.

It isn't just celebrities and physical beauty either. Consider all the different ways people judge one another. We look at titles, degrees, possessions, relative wealth, and social standing—all external attributes that have little to do with the true self.

Think of these external attributes as clothes, and it becomes clear that we are just like the doorman, dealing with others based on what they happen to be "wearing." If they drive around in a clunker, our regard for them goes down a couple of notches; if they have an advanced degree, we revise our estimate of them upward.

The trouble is that the clothes and the individual wearing them are two completely different things. For instance, we may meet a Peace Corps volunteer who does not possess much in the way of material things, and yet has a wealth of intangible treasures in the heart. Or perhaps we meet a scientist with an impressive title and academic honors—but not a single shred of common sense.

When we look beyond the surface and behold the real person, we begin to see in terms of spirituality. In this inner realm, the external attributes that we use to discriminate have no meaning. This is what Mother Teresa spoke of when she answered the question of how she was able to care for the lepers year after year. She said she saw God in them, wearing many disguises.

If we look through the eyes of the sage or Mother Teresa, we too will see the truth—the truth that we are one. As spiritual beings, we all partake in the divine essence, none higher and none lower. This eternal self is who we really are, and no matter how many different sets of clothes we change into, this is the part of us that will never change.

人不可貌相，海水不可斗量。

Chapter 17

A Conversation of Waves

Why Do We Keep Comparing Ourselves to Others?

比較之心

There was once a small wave who was unhappy. "I'm so miserable," it moaned. "The other waves are big and powerful, while I'm so little and weak. Why is life so unfair?"

Another wave passing by heard the small wave and decided to stop by. "You only think so because you haven't seen your own original nature clearly. You think you're a wave and you think you're suffering. In reality you are neither."

"What?" The small wave was surprised. "I'm not a wave? But it's obvious I'm a wave! I've got my crest, see? And there's my wake, little as it is. What do you mean I'm not a wave?"

"This thing you call 'wave' is merely a temporary form you assume for a short time. You're really just water! When you understand completely that this is your fundamental nature, you will no longer be confused about being a wave, and you will be free of your misery."

"If I'm water, what about you?"

"I'm water too. I'm temporarily assuming the form of a wave somewhat larger than you, but that doesn't change my fundamental essence—water! I'm you and you're me. We're part of a greater self."

The Tao

道

Many people, mired in the illusion known as the material world, mistakenly assume they belong only to themselves. They compare themselves to others, and if they perceive some sort of lack or inequity, they become miserable.

They would feel quite differently if they could see, as clearly as the sages can, the fundamental oneness in which we are all inextricably integrated. We are all connected to one another in a way beyond the perception of the physical senses or the explanation of science. We are, in short, part of a greater whole.

This greater self has many names—the Oversoul, Universal Consciousness, God, and so on. The moment we can see the reality of this teaching is the moment that our compulsive need to compare and compete drops away.

知足之足，常足矣。

Chapter 18

The Gong

Living Life as the Party It Was Meant to Be

銅鑼聲

Once upon a time in ancient China, there were two brothers. Both worked hard and accumulated much wealth.

One day, they were traveling on the road when it started to rain. They were still far from the next village, so they looked around for shelter. They found an abandoned temple at a nearby cemetery.

They went into the temple and saw that an old man was already inside. They noticed he held a small gong in one hand. Curious, they asked him about it.

The old man said: "I am a messenger. My job is to go to the door of people who are about to die, and strike this gong three times. It is the signal for them to pass away."

The brothers were taken aback, but then they thought the old man was most likely crazy.

Seeing their expression, the old man said: "I know what you're thinking. You don't believe me. Well, it so happens that the two of you will die next week. You can see for yourself when your time comes." Then he vanished right in front of them.

The brothers were shocked. They resumed their journey after the rain stopped, but both were disturbed by this most unusual experience.

The old man's words weighed heavily on the older brother's mind. He kept thinking, "I worked hard to accumulate all this wealth, but what's it all for? I have only a few days left, and then I will be gone." He lost his appetite and couldn't sleep. Soon he was sick.

When the day came, he was too ill to get out of bed. He heard the sound of the gong being struck three times and died, exactly as the old man said.

The old man's words also weighed heavily on the younger brother's mind. He kept thinking: "I worked hard to accumulate all this wealth, but what's it all for? I have only a few days left, and then I will be gone."

Then he thought: "There is no time to waste. I must do something with this wealth, and quickly!" He jumped into the task of divesting his possessions. He went around his village to give money to worthy causes as well as public works.

The villagers were surprised by his generosity, and also very grateful. They got together and decided to hold a celebration in his honor. They all showed up in front of his house and had a big party. Musicians played music, people danced and toasted his kindness. Everyone was having a great time.

The old man showed up with his gong. He saw that it was very crowded and noisy. He had a job to do, so he got as close to the house as possible and struck the gong three times.

No one heard him. People assumed he was one of the musicians. The younger brother was so busy talking to people, accepting their thanks, and clasping their hands that he didn't even know the old man was there.

The old man tried again. And again. He was having no luck at all. Finally he got frustrated and left.

A week later, the younger brother was busier than ever. People saw him as a community leader, and many wanted him to work with them on various projects, or get his opinions on issues of common concern.

Between appointments, the younger brother found himself wondering: "Wasn't that old man supposed to show up at my doorstep? Oh well, no time to worry about that. There are still many people I need to help."

The Tao
道

There are several teachings in this story. The old man and the gong symbolize the inevitability of life leading to death. If you think about it, we can all expect a visit from the old man at some point in the future. We may not know when he'll show up, but we do know he'll arrive sooner or later. It is a fate that none of us can escape.

We react to this in different ways. Some of us, like the older brother, bow to the inevitability of it all. It depresses us. It robs us of energy. We may not get physically sick over it, but we can certainly be afflicted by a spiritual illness. This illness manifests itself as boredom and inertia. We're bored and yet we don't want to do anything. What's the point? Why bother?

Another way to react to it is more like the younger brother. He recognized the same inevitability of the same fate, but he decided to do something about it. Rather than admit defeat, the very fact that life was limited inspired him to live it fully.

Notice that only one thought separated the two. This demonstrates the possibility that an instant of clarity, a single moment of sudden realization, can be all it takes to change one's life forever. This is the nature of enlightenment— seemingly so distant that it will always be beyond reach . . . but at the same time only a heartbeat away.

The wealth of the brothers represents all the things we accumulate as we move through life. Not just the material possessions, but also the mental baggage we drag around with us. The wealth is in fact clutter, in our environment and in the mind: the old magazines we can't throw away but will never read again; the feeling of resentment against someone from the past; and so on.

The actions of the younger brother—divesting his wealth, giving to others, contributing to the common good—are symbolic of Tao cultivation. When we cultivate the Tao, we give unconditionally, we simplify our lives, and we focus on other people instead of ourselves. The more we do this, the more spiritually powerful we become, and the more joy we experience in life.

This is exactly what we learn in the following lines from chapter 81 of *Tao Te Ching:*

Sages do not accumulate
The more they assist others, the more they possess
The more they give to others, the more they gain

These lines, considered in conjunction with the story, point to a powerful truth: Tao cultivation allows us to transcend fate. When the old man showed up at the younger brother's house, the younger brother paid him no attention—because he was giving of himself, totally focused on his guests, and fully engaged in living life to the utmost. Thus, the old man had no power over him.

It is exactly the same for us. Cultivating the Tao isn't all about solitary meditations and mountain retreats. It is also about community. It's about interacting with people, sensing our oneness with them, and feeling the invigorating energy that results from personal interaction. The more we do for others, the more blissful contentment we experience; the more we give to others, the more joyous satisfaction we receive.

When we live this teaching, life becomes the party it should be, just like the one outside the younger brother's house. When negativity shows up at your doorstep, it will have no power over you. The positive energy you have generated blocks it, so it has no choice but to leave you alone.

In fact, you wouldn't even notice that the negative karma came and left—just like the younger brother, you would be far too busy celebrating life!

既以為人己愈有，既以與人己愈多。

Chapter 19
The Lock

Unlocking the Treasure Vault of Love and Friendship

心鎖

Once upon a time there was a vault containing gold, diamonds, and gems. A sturdy lock guarded the door to this vault to keep its contents secure.

The mighty crowbar came by and saw the lock as a challenge. He had never encountered anything he couldn't demolish before. Did they really think they could keep him out of the vault with one simple lock?

The crowbar was a thick and heavy bar of iron. Countless crates, chests, and cabinets had disintegrated before his attack. He took considerable pride in his strength and destructive power. Looking at the lock, he decided he should smash it, just to make a point.

The crowbar struck the lock, expecting it to break apart, but it was unaffected.

This surprised him. He struck again, putting more force into it. He got the same result—the lock didn't even show a dent! Now he was becoming annoyed.

Using his full strength, the crowbar struck again and again. Sparks flew and the noise was deafening. When finally he stopped, exhausted, he was amazed to see that the lock was still in one piece. This was the toughest obstacle he had ever faced.

He was still trying to figure out what to do next when the key came along. He looked at the key and saw that she was very small compared to him. The difference between them was dramatic. He was massive and muscular; she seemed insignificant and weak.

She asked him: "Were you the one making all that racket?"

"Oh, you ain't heard nothing yet. Just let me catch my breath and I'll show this lock who's boss."

"No need," said the key. She slipped into the lock and turned slightly. The crowbar heard a click, and then the lock fell open.

He couldn't believe it. "Wait a minute. This makes no sense. I am a lot more powerful than you are. How can you open it so easily when I couldn't do it after all that effort?"

The key told him: "Because I am the one who understands the heart of the lock."

The Tao

道

We all encounter obstacles in life. They keep us from the things we want and frustrate us. When we come up against such obstacles, it can be very easy for us to be like the crowbar, wanting to use the brute force approach to break apart or smash through the things that stand in the way. Our language reflects this tendency: when we make significant progress with a problem, we call it a breakthrough.

All too often we find that the crowbar approach doesn't work. For instance, a salesman who encounters resistance to his pitch may resort to high-pressure sales tactics, only to meet with even more resistance. Just as it was for the crowbar, the increased effort leads to a lot of noise but little or no success.

Or consider what happens when you have a disagreement with others and you know you're right. You become ever more forceful. You hammer away at their arguments and crush their points one by one. But much to your frustration, they cling to their views even more stubbornly than before, refusing to see your logic. The interactions become strained. Eventually, like the crowbar, you have to stop because you are exhausted.

Tao sages approach such life obstacles in a very different way. From their observation of nature, they realize that the truly strong does not have the appearance of strength, and in the long run, it is always "soft" that triumphs over "hard." Thus, in chapter 43 of *Tao Te Ching* we see the following lines:

The softest things in the world
Override the hardest things in the world

For instance, water is infinitely flexible and conforms to any shape, while rocks are solid and unyielding. And yet, given time, water will invariably penetrate into, cut through, wear down, and wash away rocks.

There are numerous other examples. When the hurricane comes, it is the lowly and pliable grass that bends with the winds and survives, while the mighty but inflexible trees are uprooted and toppled. Or consider what happens when people advance into their senior years. They lose their teeth (the "hard") but their tongues (the "soft") remain the same.

When we apply this principle to human affairs, we begin to see that it isn't such a great idea to force your views on others. In an argument, the most important thing isn't being "right." You can assert your righteousness until you're blue in the face and still have no success in winning over others. In fact, you may even achieve the opposite and push people away.

In general, when we try to force an issue or force agreement, what little gains we achieve are never proportional to the work we put into it. The effort and struggles do not translate into progress. Instead, they go into increasing tension, destroying harmony, and damaging relationships.

The far better way—the way of the Tao—is to be like the key. The lock is not an obstacle to the key because the key knows its inner workings. Similarly, when faced with a problem, what we need to do is not to attack it from the outside, but to understand it from within. Once you thoroughly understand the heart of the matter, it can no longer exist as an obstacle. There will be nothing for you to smash into pieces, and nothing for you to break through.

Armed with complete understanding, it will require very little effort for you to achieve your objective. Like the slight turn of the key, your actions don't seem like much, and yet you are able to achieve agreement while reducing tension, promoting harmony, and building relationships. This is the secret of wu wei. By seemingly doing almost nothing, there is nothing that the Tao sage cannot accomplish. The sage's insight—literally the inside view—is the key to this secret.

The same principle applies not just when we encounter problems, but also when we interact with others day in and day out. Everyone's heart is like a vault, locked and kept secure by a sturdy lock. The treasures in the vault represent the heart's great potential for love, friendship, and support.

If you wish to gain access to this treasure, put away your crowbar. It doesn't matter how thick it is; it will never be able to pry open the door. Use instead the key of kindness and caring. When you insert this key, you'll find that it fits the lock perfectly. And with a slight turn of the key, all the treasures of the vault shall be yours.

天下之至柔，馳騁天下之至堅。

Chapter 20
The Water Pump

The Karmic Laws of Giving and Receiving

施與受

There was once a man who was lost in the desert. The water in his canteen had run out two days earlier, and he was on his last legs. He knew that if he didn't get some water soon, he would surely perish.

The man saw a shack ahead of him. He thought it might be a mirage or hallucination, but having no other option, he moved toward it. As he got closer he realized it was quite real, so he dragged his weary body to the door with the last of his strength.

The shack was not occupied and seemed to have been abandoned for quite some time. The man gained entrance, hoping against hope that he might find water inside.

His heart skipped a beat when he saw what was in the shack: a water pump. It had a pipe going down through the floor, perhaps tapping a source of water deep underground.

He began working the pump, but no water came out. He kept at it and still nothing happened. Finally he gave up from exhaustion and frustration. He threw up his hands in despair. It looked as if he was going to die after all.

Then the man noticed a bottle in one corner of the shack. It was filled with water and corked up to prevent evaporation.

He uncorked the bottle and was about to gulp down the sweet life-giving water when he noticed a piece of paper attached to it. Handwriting on the paper read: "Use this water to start the pump. Don't forget to fill the bottle when you're done."

He had a dilemma. He could follow the instructions and pour the water into the pump, or he could ignore it and just drink the water.

What to do? If he let the water go into the pump, what assurance did he have that it would work? What if the pump malfunctioned? What if the pipe had a leak? What if the underground reservoir had long dried up?

But then . . . maybe the instructions were correct. Should he risk it? If they turned out to be false, he would be throwing away the last water he would ever see.

Hands trembling, he poured the water into the pump. Then he closed his eyes, said a prayer, and started working the pump.

He heard a gurgling sound, and then water came gushing out, more than he could possibly use. He luxuriated in the cool and refreshing stream. He was going to live!

After drinking his fill and feeling much better, he looked around the shack. He found a pencil and a map of the region. The map showed that he was still far away from civilization, but at least now he knew where he was and which direction to go.

He filled his canteen for the journey ahead. He also filled the bottle and put the cork back in. Before leaving, he added his own writing below the instruction: "Believe me, it works!"

The Tao

道

In chapter 51 of *Tao Te Ching*, we see these intriguing lines toward the end:

> *Produces but does not possess*
> *Acts but does not flaunt*
> *Nurtures but does not dominate*
> *This is called mystic virtue*

These lines describe how the Tao works in our plane of existence:

- *Although the Tao is the source of everything, it is not possessive of anything.*
- *Although the Tao process is actively engaged in the workings of the universe, it does not flaunt the wondrous results it achieves.*
- *Although the Tao nurtures all living things through the miracle of life, it makes no attempt to rule over them or dominate them.*

These descriptions seem quite clear, but it is not obvious why we should call them "mystic virtue." What Lao Tzu describes does not seem difficult to understand or particularly mysterious. What is so mystical about it?

The essence of mystic virtue that encompasses all the descriptions is this: the Tao gives of itself without any expectations.

Although the Tao does not expect rewards or recognition of any sort, in the middle of the chapter we see the following:

Therefore all things respect the Tao and value virtue
The respect for Tao, the value of virtue
Not due to command but to constant nature

So the Tao is revered even though it has no expectations or requirements for special treatment. For instance, the Tao manifests in living things as life, and all living things treasure the life within them. This is not because they are commanded to do so, but because it is the natural thing to do.

We begin to see the deeper meaning in this chapter when we take Lao Tzu's macroscopic view and apply it to our personal interactions with others. What will happen if we emulate the Tao by giving of ourselves to others without any expectations? This chapter suggests that we will be amply rewarded even though we expect nothing.

Furthermore, Lao Tzu is saying that this will happen naturally, because it is a principle that operates like natural laws—its results are consistent, predictable, and all but guaranteed.

The story echoes this teaching by showing us that we must give before we can receive abundantly. More important, it also teaches that faith plays an important role in giving. The man did not know if his action would be rewarded, but he proceeded regardless. Without knowing what to expect, he made a leap of faith.

Water in this story represents the good things in life. Think of it as positive energy, or something that brings a smile to your face. It can be material objects or intangible qualities. It can represent money, love, friendship, happiness, respect, or any number of other things you value. Whatever it is that you would like to get out of life, that's water.

The water pump represents the workings of the karmic mechanism. Give it some water to work with, and it will return far more than you put in. This mechanism traces a great circle, an unbroken path that eventually comes back to its point of origin. The energy of this circulation gathers power as it moves along, so that when it finally returns, it is greatly amplified.

If the circle is a physical phenomenon, like the orbit of a planet or the cycle of seasons, then we can follow its path, observe its progress, and predict when the circle will be complete. We cannot do so with the karmic mechanism, because it is metaphysical in nature. Karma weaves its way in and out of the physical world with the greatest of ease, and when it goes into the nonphysical realm, it disappears from view.

This is why we cannot always see the connection between cause and effect. If you perform a good deed and receive immediate praise as a result, the karmic relationship is easy to understand. The circle, in this case, is relatively small.

More often than not, the circle is so vast that we lose track of it. Perhaps you have done a good deed that no one knows about, so you assume there will not be an effect associated with this particular cause. In reality, you have but initiated the karmic mechanism in the spiritual realm. You cannot see it, but it is there all the same, and it begins gathering energy and seeking its way back to you immediately.

At some point in the future, this unseen positive karma will emerge in the material world to continue on its circular path back to you. When that happens, it will seem as if it materializes out of nowhere; it will look like a causeless effect. You may even wonder about this good fortune that comes from such an unexpected direction, not realizing you are in fact its original source.

Now we begin to see why Lao Tzu calls this "mystic virtue." Its workings are indeed mystical and mysterious. If we emulate the Tao and create positive energy—give of ourselves—without expectations, the universe will reciprocate in kind on a massive scale. This remains true even when we cannot see the connection between the original giving and the subsequent reciprocation.

If you find this difficult to accept, then recall the basic concept that at a fundamental level of reality, everything is connected with everything else. There is no true separation, no clearly defined boundaries between anything. If we can keep this in mind, the mystic virtue may not seem quite as strange as before. All are part of the oneness we call Tao. The separation that we perceive in the material world is but an illusion.

As we have already noted from the story, the man filled the pump without knowing if his effort would be rewarded. In the same way, when we emulate the Tao and nurture others, we also act without expecting rewards of any sort.

It is a principle that applies to everything, not just money. For instance, in order to win the respect of others, one must start by giving others the appropriate respect without quibbles or qualms.

Would you like more recognition for the work that you do? If so, then start by recognizing the achievements of everyone around you. When you truly accept that others are deserving of recognition, their esteem for you will increase as if by magic.

Would you like to have more friendship in your life? If so, then start by being friendly. Do not expect anything in return, and you'll be pleasantly surprised by the flood of goodwill and friendliness that comes your way.

Would you like people to see beauty in you? If so, then start noticing beauty in others. It's easy to see when you pay attention. Everyone around you has an intrinsic beauty that goes well beyond the physical. When you can see this and start to appreciate it and marvel at it, a transformation takes place: you become truly beautiful yourself.

In general, whatever goodness you want from life, give it to others first. Give it cheerfully and willingly, without calculating your gain versus loss as if you are working a balance sheet. Initiate the circular exchange and relax in the certain knowledge that no one ever gets shortchanged by the Tao process.

At this point, you may be wondering if this principle is a paradox of sorts. If we know that we will be amply rewarded without fail by creating something positive in the world, wouldn't that be an expectation? And wouldn't the expectation short-circuit the process?

Think of planting flower seeds in a garden as a metaphor for the karmic mechanism. Each seed you plant is a process you have set into motion. You understand the principles that govern the growth of plants and you know the soil is fertile, so you know that you will see results in the fullness of time. You do not know exactly when or how the flowers will bloom, and that's perfectly fine.

Having expectations in this context means becoming attached to a specific outcome. If you insist upon the flowers blooming at an exact time in some exact shape, you are certain to be disappointed. If, in your obsession, you sit there and watch a particular flower grow, the rest of your garden is certain to be neglected.

Karma is exactly the same. You initiate the positive energy without knowing exactly how or when the effects will manifest themselves. Because you understand the karmic mechanism, you realize it will result in something good headed your way sooner or later. However, you have no attachments to any particular outcomes, and therefore no specific expectations.

Let us underscore the role of faith in all this. Just as we know the soil in the garden is fertile, we have faith in the basic benevolence of the universe. The Tao nurtures us and protects us. In a very real sense, the world wants us to succeed.

The only thing we need is the courage to take charge and jump-start the water pump.

Believe me, it works!

是以萬物莫不尊道而貴德。

Chapter 21
The Tall Hat

The Role That Flattery Plays

高帽子

In ancient China, the government ran on the Confucian system, where bureaucrats were chosen from the ranks of Confucian students based on their performance in an official exam.

Two students had done well in this exam and won government posts in a city far away. They were visiting with their teacher, to ask for his leave and also to solicit his advice, in accordance with the customs of the period.

The teacher told them: "In our society today, if you are too bluntly honest or too direct, you will surely encounter obstacles. So, when you interact with others, give them the tall hat and things will go much more smoothly."

The students understood the teacher's meaning. Headgear signified one's position *in society. Government officials wore elaborate hats indicating to their level of authority. Thus, to give someone the tall hat would be to presume in him a high level of power, thereby flattering him.*

"You are right, Master." One of the students nodded in agreement. "As I look at the world today, I see very few people out there who dislike tall hats as you do."

The teacher was enormously pleased by this remark.

They continued to exchange a few more pleasantries, and then it was time for the students to leave. As soon as they got out of the teacher's house—and earshot— the student who spoke turned to his classmate and asked: "So, what do you think of the first tall hat I handed out?"

The Tao

道

In chapter 22 of *Tao Te Ching*, we find the following four lines about the behavior of a sage:

Without flaunting themselves—and so are seen clearly
Without presuming themselves—and so are distinguished

Without praising themselves—and so have merit
Without boasting about themselves—and so are lasting

In chapter 24, we find the same idea expressed with almost the exact same words:

Those who flaunt themselves are not clear
Those who presume themselves are not distinguished
Those who praise themselves have no merit
Those who boast about themselves do not last

Given the overall brevity and terseness of the *Tao Te Ching*, this repetition is remarkable and interesting. It's a cue to us that this is an important lesson, so we should pay extra attention to it.

Many people may think that this is an easy lesson to master, since they do not see themselves as show-offs. They may be the shy type who do are not normally flaunting, presumptuous, or boastful, so they feel they have nothing new to learn here. If we look just a little deeper, though, we'll see that reality is not quite that simple, because the ego's need to elevate itself takes many subtle forms.

For instance, it is very easy for Tao practitioners to see themselves as head and shoulders above people who are ignorant of the Tao. Because Tao philosophy is more sophisticated, elegant, and consistent than other belief systems, we tend to assume—without any other basis—that it makes us superior somehow. We are presumptuous even if we don't externalize it with words or actions. This is something most of us will recognize in our hearts if we are brutally honest with ourselves.

The story is rich with irony. The teacher lamented the common people's weakness for flattery without realizing that he himself was just as susceptible. Because he saw himself as being above other people, he became a prime target for the tall hat. His self-elevation above the masses was the very thing that lowered him back down to the same level.

The point of this story is especially important to those of us who are on the path of cultivation. If we feel superior for having learned the lesson of humility, well . . . we really haven't learned anything at all!

The teacher was the type of person who praised himself. In his mind, he was already convinced of his own virtues. He would never say it out loud, of course—that would be too obviously immodest. What he did not realize was that his internal self-praise was already obvious to the students. He was blind to a tailor-made tall hat, because it matched his own private thoughts exactly, and therefore passed right through his critical faculties.

The *Tao Te Ching* tells us that such a person has no real merit, because his inflated self-image is based on insecurities rather than true capabilities. Someone who has not accomplished much tends to be quite eager for others to know everything about his little achievements. Conversely, someone who is truly accomplished probably doesn't have much interest in elevating himself, because his focus is on his work and not on self-promotion.

It seems to be a permanent part of human nature that we will always be able to see other people much more clearly than we can see ourselves. This is how we can perceive the lack of substance in a braggart, and the real value in someone who does much more than he or she claims. Slick talk and fancy footwork may obscure the truth for a while, but sooner or later we figure it out. This is why show-offs do not last.

Be cautious about your ego's tendency to position yourself too high, especially if you think the teaching from the two chapters is an easy lesson to master. The teacher from our story did not see himself as a show-off or braggart either, and yet he stood revealed as the very opposite of who he thought he was. There's a lot we can learn from his example!

信言不美，美言不信。

Chapter 22
The Eight Winds

How Friends Help One Another Deal with Ego

八風

Su Dongpo, one of the great Chinese poets who lived about a thousand years ago, in the Song dynasty, was an avid student of Buddhist teachings. He often discussed Buddhism with his good friend, the Zen master Foyin. The two lived across the river from each other—Su Dongpo's residence on the north side and Foyin's Gold Mountain Temple on the south side.

One day, Su Dongpo felt inspired and wrote the following poem:

I bow my head to the heaven within heaven
Hairline rays illuminating the universe

The eight winds cannot move me
Sitting still upon the purple golden lotus

Impressed by himself, Su Dongpo dispatched a servant to hand-carry this poem to Foyin. He felt certain that his friend would be just as impressed.

When Foyin read the poem, he immediately saw that it was both a tribute to the Buddha and a declaration of spiritual refinement. The "eight winds" in the poem referred to praise, ridicule, honor, disgrace, gain, loss, pleasure, and misery— interpersonal forces of the material world that drove and influenced the hearts of men. Su Dongpo was saying that he had attained a higher level of spirituality, where these forces no longer affected him.

Smiling, the Zen master wrote "fart" on the manuscript and had it returned to Su Dongpo.

Su Dongpo had been expecting compliments and a seal of approval, so he was shocked when he saw what the Zen master had written. He hit the roof: "How dare he insult me like this? Why that lousy old monk! He's got a lot of explaining to do!"

Full of indignation, Su Dongpo ordered a boat to ferry him to the other shore as quickly as possible. Once there, he jumped off and charged into the temple. He wanted to find Foyin and demand an apology.

He found Foyin's door closed. On the door was a piece of paper, with the following two lines:

The eight winds cannot move me
One fart blows me across the river

This stopped Su Dongpo cold. Foyin had anticipated this hotheaded visit. Su Dongpo's anger suddenly drained away as he understood his friend's meaning. If he really was a man of spiritual refinement, completely unaffected by the eight winds, then how could he be so easily provoked?

With a few strokes of the pen and minimal effort, Foyin showed that Su Dongpo was in fact not as spiritually advanced as he claimed to be. Ashamed but wiser, Su Dongpo departed quietly.

This event proved to be a turning point in Su Dongpo's spiritual development. From that point on, he became a man of humility, and not merely someone who claimed to possess the virtue.

The Tao

道

One of the most difficult lessons to master is transcending the ego. On an intellectual level, we can understand all the reasoning behind the lesson, but when the time comes to walk the walk and not just talk the talk, our actions often fall short of the ideals we envision.

The ego tends to manifest itself as a powerful urge to be right. Its effect is insidious—we are usually unaware of it when it exerts its influence over us. It is a negative force because it does not compel us to seek deeper truths or further clarifications. Instead, it takes the shortcut of twisting our thoughts until we become convinced of our own correctness.

Armed with this conviction, we launch into a manic drive to prove a point, to win at any cost. Sometimes our position matches objective reality; other times it does not. Blinded by the ego, we cannot see the difference between the two. And even if we are ultimately proven correct, the victory will feel hollow and empty, because it is obtained at the expense of harmony and compassion.

We can remind ourselves to keep the ego in check, but the moment someone attacks our views, we immediately discard the reminder and jump right back into the fray. It is as if we are not truly in charge . . . as if our actions and words are the slaves of the trigger-happy, contentious ego.

Su Dongpo's story tells us that managing one's ego seems to be a perpetual human challenge, as tricky a thousand years ago as it is today. If even the great Su Dongpo had trouble with it, then of course mere mortals like ourselves would have at least some issues.

The story made a clear distinction between knowing a truth and living it. Su Dongpo's mental brilliance was beyond question, noted by his contemporaries and those of subsequent generations who studied his poems. In all likelihood, he really did understand the eight winds very well. Unfortunately, this was an intellectual understanding that did not translate into correct action or appropriate inaction.

In the same way, our understanding of the ego also does not translate into the ability to control it. Without true mastery, and merely knowing the reasoning behind the lesson on a rational level, we continue to make the same mistakes again and again. Being able to see a path is not the same as walking it.

The ego operates within a social context. Su Dongpo sought peer approval because he craved praise and admiration, which was in turn because the ego is all about "looking good" to others. We can think of it as a mask that we put on to play a certain role in life. This mask comes off when we are alone—away from the social context—because then we don't have a need to cut a dashing figure for the sake of appearance.

This means the total elimination of the ego may not be a realistic goal. As social creatures, most of us will always need and seek out the company of other human beings. Some measure of ego will always be present as long as human interactions persist, no matter how saintly the participants of such interactions may be.

Perhaps this is the key. Can it be that we give ourselves an impossible task if we think we have to get rid of the ego somehow? What would happen if we focus our goal on freedom instead of elimination?

Ego enslaves us by making us too dependent on what other people think. We become easily incensed when we fail to get the approval or concurrence we expect. When that happens, it is easy for ego to control us because of our overwhelming need to be seen by others as being correct.

If we were to give in to the ego's craving for attention, we would quickly find that it can never be satisfied. An entertainer can be the idol of millions and the center of adulation in a stadium full of fans and still feel utterly alone. Once the ego grows out of balance, it can easily become a bottomless hole, forever wanting more.

Thus, by freedom from ego, we do not mean extinction of the ego in the Buddhist sense, nor are we talking about suppressing it or denying its existence. Suppression and denial are among the least effective ways of dealing with the ego. To be free from the ego simply means breaking away from its grip so we are not enslaved by its domination. We want to master the ego, and not be its servants.

This means letting go of the need to defend. We relinquish the desire to convince or persuade others. We can hold on to our views without having to make any points, prove anything, or justify any positions. When we free ourselves from this falsehood, we gain clarity. We begin to see that being defensive is a tremendous waste of energy that achieves nothing useful. Our views do not gain any validity when we defend them, nor do they lose any validity when we choose not to defend.

知者不博，博者不知。

PART FOUR

With Family

家庭

The Chinese have a saying: "When the family is harmonious, everything prospers."

The importance of one's family cannot be emphasized enough. It is your home base, your safe harbor, your castle. It is where you rest, heal, and grow; it can also be a source of tremendous strength.

The relationships we create and maintain within the family have a direct impact outside of it. Happiness at home tends to be reflected as success in the community and the workplace. Conversely, discord at home often leads to failures and misfortunes in other aspects of life. Thus, Tao cultivators regard the family unit as an essential setting for cultivation.

How do we create, improve, and maintain harmony in the family? Tao cultivators use the following as general guidelines:

- *Are there arguments in the family? If so, remember that everyone has his or her own perspective.*

- *Is a family member being particularly difficult? If so, remember that he or she is a valuable resource, and there is always a way to learn from a resource.*
- *Is someone in the family accumulating possessions but not taking the time to enjoy them? If so, it's time to stop and think about what is more important in life.*
- *How do you regard the people in your family? Are you able to see them as living Buddhas?*
- *Is there too much clutter at home, disrupting the harmony of the family? If so, what are your attachments that lead to this clutter?*

Chapter 23

You Are Right

Maintaining a Harmonious Atmosphere

你是對的

One day, the sage was having tea with the disciple when they heard a commotion outside. Two men were arguing about something. Their volume got louder and louder. Neither side was willing to back down.

After much shouting, one of them stalked off in anger. The remaining man stood seething. After a while, he came inside to look for the sage.

"Master, you must resolve this issue for us," he said. "I tried to reason with him, but he wouldn't listen. He is extremely stubborn."

The sage indicated his willingness to help, and the man went on to describe the argument. He explained in meticulous detail why his position was obviously the most reasonable and most correct.

"So what do you say, Master? Am I right, or is he right?" the man asked.

"Of course you are right!" The sage said. The man beamed, and left in a good mood.

Moments later, the man who had stalked off before came back, also looking for the sage.

"Master, you probably heard me arguing a while ago," he said. "The other fellow's position is based entirely on false logic, while my statements are backed up by solid evidence. Can you resolve this issue for us?"

The sage nodded, and the man presented his side of the story. He carefully pointed out all the flaws in his opponent's thinking and listed all the proofs supporting his position.

"What do you think, Master? Who's right and who's wrong?" the man asked.

"Of course you are right!" the sage said. The man beamed, and left in a good mood.

The disciple, who had remained silent all this time, couldn't help but express his puzzlement: "Master, how can this be? If he is right, then the other man is wrong, but you already told the other man he was right, so this one must be wrong! One position is true, while the opposite is false. They cannot both be true! Am I right?"

"Of course you are right!" the sage said.

The Tao
道

The only way we can approach the Tao is to relax the death grip of logic, and engage the far more powerful tool of intuition. When the rationality of the brain utterly fails to grasp the Tao, the heart will step in to embrace it with a way of knowing that is beyond knowledge. Feeling is the key.

Wanting to be right is one of our major obsessions in life. We seem to have a desperate need to prove ourselves correct at any cost. If someone disagrees, we expend tremendous physical and emotional energies to force them to see things our way. We argue with them.

Does it work? Usually not. Arguments rarely bring agreement. Most of the time, they drive us apart. You can have the most rigorous reasoning and the most solid supporting evidence imaginable and still fail to convince the other party, because arguments aren't really about the truth. They are about the very human need to be right—regardless of facts.

This is why sages refrain from arguments. Arguing requires much effort but delivers poor results. The more you force a different view on people, the more they resist. Thus, arguments and debates are usually the very opposite of wu wei.

Chapter 81 of *Tao Te Ching* expresses this clearly:

Those who are good do not debate
Those who debate are not good

It isn't that sages suppress or deny the urge to argue. They transcend it. They can see the futility in imposing their opinions on an unwilling audience. Since it's a waste of energy, they direct their attention away from it to being perceptive to perspectives other than their own.

Because they are detached and observant, sages have the ability to move freely among multiple points of view. Most people can see the truth only from their side. To the sages, such a limited perspective is like having blinders on. The sages' expanded perception allows them to see how two sides can both be right. In fact, they recognize that there are as many valid perspectives as there are people in the world, and every perspective is valid to someone somewhere.

The conventional concept of absolute right and wrong is illusory. It may be comforting to those who need a simplified, black-and-white view of a complex reality with many shades of gray, but it can also lead to inflexibility, closed-mindedness, dogma, and even fanaticism.

It isn't that the sages have no opinions of their own. Quite the opposite. Not only do sages have opinions, these opinions tend to be exceptionally well-informed precisely because they are able to see things from many angles. Thus, far from not knowing right from wrong, the sages are rigorous and disciplined in maintaining their personal notions of right and wrong.

The crucial key is that the sages are just as rigorous and disciplined in refraining from imposing their notions upon those who are unreceptive. After all, why should the sage argue with you when you are right?

善者不辯，辯者不善。

Chapter 24
The Resource

How to See Others as Valuable and Lovable Resources

師與資

Therefore the good person is the teacher of the bad person
The bad person is the resource of the good person
Those who do not value their teachers
And do not love their resources
Although intelligent, they are greatly confused

The Tao

道

The above, from chapter 27 of *Tao Te Ching,* has much to do with a cliché that we often hear: when you point a finger at someone else, three of your fingers point back at yourself. The same sentiment has been expressed in many different ways. For instance, we have the familiar expression that one who lives in a glass house should not throw rocks. We need to realize our own imperfection and not be so quick to judge others. Jesus took this a step further and questioned why we should judge at all. He expressed this with the immortal phrase: "He who is without sin, let him cast the first stone."

When we seek faults in others, we are pointing the finger of accusation. We're also throwing stones of recrimination and blame. All too often we do so without thinking about our own faults. We cannot see the glass house in which we live.

This is something most of us can agree on, but few of us can put into practice. Pointing fingers isn't just limited to blaming and accusing. It is also a way to highlight shortcomings in others, to mock and to criticize. We seem to enjoy doing this too much to ever give it up.

Even now, as you think about specific examples from your life, you may be able to see the problem. We all see certain faults in others that we simply cannot stand. Sometimes it can be hard to resist the temptation to say a few choice words about them—you may regret it later, but venting a bit really gives you a momentary satisfaction, doesn't it?

"I'm only telling the truth," you may say in your own defense. "The negative things I'm pointing out are exactly the way they are. Really, this person deserves a lot more than the little bit I have dished out."

In other words, you have cast yourself in the role of the protagonist; your target is, of course, the antagonist in your little life drama.

Remember that in the Tao paradigm everything is relative. Everything has meaning only in comparison with something else. What that means in this case is that you are not always the "good person." You may be, compared to someone who hasn't caught up to your level of personal development, but compared to someone else who's more spiritually refined, you are suddenly the "bad person."

We can see how a bad person may have much to learn, thus making a teacher out of the good person. But how can the bad person be a resource to the good person? What does Lao Tzu mean by that?

One way the bad person can be a resource is to serve as an example. The good benefits from the bad through observation. For instance, when an ignorant individual has done something unwise that causes a lot of trouble, you want to observe and learn in order to avoid repeating the same mistake.

Another way the bad person can be a resource is to serve as a mirror and a magnifier. The crucial insight here is that the fault that you find so repulsive in someone else most likely exists in you as well. It may be only a trace, or it may be a problem you've had in the past, or it may be a potential that you fear. The more you dislike it in yourself, the more violently you react to someone else who exhibits the same attribute. It is as if you are seeing yourself in a funhouse mirror, with some negativity reflected and magnified. It is something that can really drive you nuts.

A good friend of mine had an experience with this at a most visceral level. He was heading down the street one day when he saw an overweight woman with rotten teeth struggling with her children. The scene struck him as an incredibly repulsive sight.

It bothered him a great deal, and he couldn't get rid of the mental image for the rest of the day. He finally decided to talk to someone about it. A friend of his had a deep understanding of psychology, so he turned to this gentleman and expressed his feelings of disgust and revulsion against the woman.

His friend was silent for a time. And then he asked: "Did you ever have a weight problem?"

"Yes. I used to be badly out of shape."

"How about your teeth? Did you ever have problems with your teeth?"

"I had a lot of dental work done—ah, I see where you're going with this."

His friend nodded. "And kids? Any trouble with kids in the past?"

"Yes," he replied, and began to understand. "It really wasn't her I disliked so much. All along, it was me, or perhaps my fear of the potential in me to become like her. No wonder it got to me so much."

You can see the same thing for yourself. I recommend that you try the following exercise: Make a list of the people you dislike. Next to each name, write down the characteristic of the person that really bugs you. Then go through the list of faults and be brutally honest. You may find, much to your chagrin, that every fault you have written exists in some fashion, at some point in time, within yourself.

Don't let this get you down. Instead, realize that these people have done you a favor. They serve a useful function in highlighting the imperfections in your character. They have become, literally, valuable resources.

Also, keep in mind that a sense of humor has always been part of the Tao. It is very Tao-like for us to have a little fun while we cultivate spirituality. With that in mind, let us utilize this insight in creative ways.

Go to the people you dislike, and tell them, with complete sincerity, that they have been a great resource to you. Can you just imagine their incredulous facial expression when they hear this from you?

Have your loved ones read this chapter—or better yet, explain it to them in your own words. Next time you have a fight with them, and you know you're in the wrong but can't bring yourself to apologize (gentlemen, pay special attention), ask them if you have just been a great resource. This will dissolve the tension instantaneously.

Let's reexamine the cliché with which we began this discussion—when you point a finger at someone else, three of your fingers point back at yourself. We have seen that this is literally true because the fault that you dislike in someone invariably exists in some form within yourself. Perhaps it's only a trace, but it's there nonetheless, and you react to it.

What happens when you are truly without any faults? Well, none of your fingers would be pointing back at all. Thus, as you extend your hand toward the one with the faults, all of your fingers are pointing in the same direction toward that person. Visualize this in your mind.

Notice your gesture is no longer one of accusation or indictment. Instead, you are reaching out to offer either a handshake or a helping hand. With none of your fingers able to point back, it is simply not possible for you to seek faults with finger pointing. The person at fault is your resource, and you love your resource . . . for you have become the teacher.

善人者，不善人之師；不善人者，善人之資。

Chapter 25

Possession and Enjoyment

How Material Things Can Get in the Way of Joy

擁有與享受

It was a beautiful day. The sky was clear and the temperature was pleasantly cool, so the sage decided to take a walk.

By chance, his walk took him near a luxurious house. It belonged to a wealthy man the sage knew well. In front of it was a beautiful garden filled with exotic flowers imported from distant lands.

As the sage drew closer, he saw that many of these flowers were in full bloom. He could not help but admire their beauty. Their colors were so vivid and vibrant—almost leaping off the petals in their brilliance.

The sage marveled at the human ingenuity that managed to transplant these flowers from so far away—probably some tropical paradise he had never visited.

He stood for a few minutes to savor the sight. He breathed deeply to take in the fragrance. After a while, he let out a contended sigh and continued on his way.

The sage thought about the wealthy man. He had recently become very ill. They were old friends, so the sage was quite concerned.

The doctor said the illness was caused by stress. The man suffered from too much tension in managing his business. This business was the source of his wealth, but he paid for success dearly—with his health.

The problem was that the man insisted on doing everything himself, taking on ever more responsibilities. As the pressure mounted, he lost his appetite and could no longer get a good night's sleep. He was constantly fatigued and lost interest in the simple pleasures of life.

In fact, the gentleman had neglected the garden for many years. He lacked the time, energy, and inclination to walk among the beautiful flowers in his own garden.

Suddenly, the irony of it all became apparent. The wealthy man owned the garden but could not enjoy it. The sage did not own it, and yet was able to enjoy it fully.

The Tao

道

One of the most typical misconceptions in life revolves around possession and enjoyment as they relate to happiness. The confusion happens because we usually possess in order to enjoy. We purchase a DVD player in order to watch movies; we acquire a stereo in order to listen to music. Possession and enjoyment seem to go hand in hand, so we think of them together.

In reality, the two are independent of each other. Only one of them is linked to happiness, and it is not possession. Not only is possession unnecessary in order to enjoy, it can even get in the way. But many people do not look at it that way. They link possession rather than enjoyment to happiness—the exact opposite of reality.

For instance, I know a lady who associates the acquisition of jewelry with happiness. She loves rings, necklaces, and bracelets. She has a large collection, but she never wears any of it, because she fears possible theft or loss. The collection is much too precious to be exposed to risk!

The only time she is ever happy is shortly before and after a new acquisition. Buying jewelry gives her a fleeting moment of thrill, and then the hunger to acquire more returns, mercilessly driving her toward the next purchase.

You may know someone like her. Perhaps you know a car buff who has a vintage vehicle in his garage. He has spared no effort in fixing and tuning its components; he never tires of buffing and shining it—but he hardly ever drives it.

Perhaps you know someone who has a vast collection of music, but has listened to only a small fraction of it. Why? Because he's too busy looking for new CDs to complete his collection.

Perhaps you know someone who has just upgraded her living room with brand new, color-coordinated couches and loveseats. She keeps the clear plastic covers on them because she doesn't want the beautiful furniture to get stained or gather dust. When you visit her and sit in her living room, you find yourself literally on plastic. You have to be careful to not move too much or you risk creating rude noises.

Perhaps you know a friend in a relationship who is focusing on possessing, rather than enjoying, the other person. If your friend continues down that path without realizing what's going on, you know the relationship will probably fail.

You can see that the one single thread that runs through all of the above examples is the emphasis on possession over enjoyment. If you look around in an observant frame of mind, you will see many more examples. For instance, when

I look at my bookshelves, I see many books. Each book is a beautiful flower of wisdom, waiting to be savored. What I already possess is a garden full of flowers, but like the wealthy man, I've been neglecting it. Instead of enjoying them, I've been going to the bookstore to get more. Endless acquisition has become a habit.

If we break this habitual pattern, we can be doing ourselves a tremendous favor. The energy and time we wasted before can now be freed up. By directing them toward using and appreciating what we have, we improve the quality of life and seize the key to happiness.

There are many "gardens" in your life. You may own some or many of them, but that is an unimportant detail. The important thing—the only thing—is that you can enjoy them, if you really want to.

Let us direct our attention to the flowers in these gardens. When you breathe in their fragrance and take in their dazzling colors, you cannot help but marvel at the miracle of human existence. It is a miracle that has brought a piece of the heavenly paradise into our mortal plane. It is the Tao.

金玉滿堂，莫之能守。

Chapter 26
The Buddha in Your Home

Have We Been Taking Loved Ones for Granted?

家中活佛

Once upon a time in ancient China, a young man by the name of Yang Fu said good-bye to his parents and embarked on a trip to Szechwan. His goal was to visit the Bodhisattva Wuji. On his way there, he encountered an old monk.

"Where are you going?" the monk inquired. Yang Fu replied that he was going to study under Bodhisattva Wuji.

"Seeking the Bodhisattva cannot compare to seeking the Buddha," asserted the old man. Yang Fu agreed with this, for although Bodhisattva Wuji was a person of great wisdom, the Buddha was the absolute paragon of enlightenment for which there was no equal.

Yang Fu then asked the old monk where he could find Buddha, and the old monk surprised him by telling him that the Buddha was at that moment in the house he left not too long ago—his own home!

Yang Fu wondered how he would recognize the Buddha. The old monk had the answer to that one as well: "When you get home, you'll see someone wearing a blanket with shoes on backward coming to greet you. That is the Buddha."

Something about the old monk's certainty convinced Yang Fu, and so he hurried home. By the time he got there, it was already the middle of the night.

His mother had already gone to bed, but when she heard her son knocking on the door, she was beside herself with happiness. Like all parents, she had been worried about her child's safety on such a long journey. She rushed out to greet him immediately. She grabbed her blanket rather than put on a coat, and in her joyful haste was totally oblivious to the fact that she had put on her slippers the wrong way.

Yang Fu took one look at his elderly mother and saw the look of pure joy on her face. Recalling to mind the monk's words, he suddenly became enlightened.

The Tao

道

Bodhi means "great awakening" or "enlightenment"; *sattva* means "being." A Bodhisattva therefore is someone who possesses great wisdom or compassion.

A wholesome thought from within the mind, a simple delight in a simple thing . . . these things are the essence of the Tao. They help us transcend the limits of our mortal selves and material obsessions.

Something uncomplicated yet profound, like the joy that radiates from a mother's heart to her child, requires no great understanding of sutras or great knowledge of Tao lore. And yet, because such a thing taps into the Tao at such a basic level, it cannot help but be filled with an elemental power.

Look at your loved ones . . . really look at them. Look deeply into their eyes. There, too, you will find the essence of the Buddha, and of the Tao.

夫孝，德之本也，教之所由生也。

Chapter 27

Master's Teacup

Dealing with Attachments to Worldly Objects
師父的茶杯

Zen Master Ikkyu had always been quick in his thinking. This quickness often came in handy when he got in trouble as a young monk. In one such occasion, Ikkyu accidentally dropped his master's teacup, breaking it into many pieces.

It was a serious problem, because the teacup was his master's favorite. It was a rare treasure, beautifully crafted from precious material. Of all of the master's possessions, it was probably the one thing he cherished the most—and now it was hopelessly smashed!

Ikkyu felt guilty, but before he could formulate a plan to get away, he heard footsteps approaching. He swept the broken pieces together and, blocking them from view with his body, turned to face the door just as the master entered.

When they were within speaking distance, Ikkyu asked: "Master, why must people die?"

His master replied: "It is perfectly natural. Everything in the world experiences both life and death."

"Everything?"

"Everything."

"So it is not something we should feel upset about?"

"Definitely not."

At that point, the crafty Ikkyu moved aside to present the broken pieces. "Master . . . your cup has experienced its inevitable death."

The Tao

道

As we smile at how young Ikkyu deftly extricated himself from trouble, the story has subtly delivered the real lesson. It sinks in at some level that material objects have a life span too, just like living beings. If we can recognize our own mortality, then surely we can also see the impermanence of our various acquisitions. They can leave us at any time, no matter how much we value them and try to hold on to them.

Most of us are quite attached to our material possessions, and will continue to cling to them even after hearing the above story and comprehending its message. We all get upset when things belonging to us are lost, damaged, or stolen. Protecting them from harm and hiding them from theft seem to give us a measure of peace—at least temporarily.

Many of us are pack rats. We accumulate boxes full of stuff that we haven't looked at or used in years. As time elapses, we find ourselves unable to recall the contents of some boxes. We forget much of what we own, so those boxes may as well not exist. And yet we refuse to dispose of them.

As the quantity of the items increases, our working and living environments become more and more cluttered. We try to fight off the encroaching chaos, but things never seem to stay organized very long. This is a major consequence of our inability to let go. Slowly but surely, we are drowning in a flood of clutter.

Perhaps we realize this is a problem, so we buy books and tapes on organization—but we succeed only in adding to the clutter with them. We seek external solutions while sinking ever deeper into the quagmire because we do not understand that we already have everything we need within ourselves.

We do not know how the master reacted to the young monk's ploy to escape accountability. If he could not let go, then the incident would bring him much misery—anger at Ikkyu's carelessness and sadness about the loss of something so valuable. If he truly practiced what he preached, and saw clearly the similarity between the "life expectancy" of material objects and human life spans, he would be able to let go of the teacup and accept the loss with perfect composure.

This connection between material possessions and the weighty issue of life and death is a new angle. It makes us realize that however difficult we find letting things go, if we were to suddenly pass on for any reason, we would have no choice but to let everything go all at once. No choice at all.

Nor is death the only thing that can separate us from our cherished belongings. Any disaster, major or minor, can do the job. If the house catches fire somehow and burns to the ground, we would have no choice but to kiss most of our possessions good-bye.

This leads us to the next question: Why wait? Why must we wait until we have no choice to learn to let go in a painful way? Why should we wait until the final moments on the deathbed, or perhaps the verge of a disaster, to gain clarity? Why do we not start letting go now?

When we truly understand this, the clutter will begin to vanish. We may notice that we have more energy in a clutter-free work environment. When clutter is present, the mind needs to tune them out. This requires mental energy—a relatively small amount, but a constant effort that, over an hour or two, could add up to quite a drain. Chances are, most of us never suspect how much pressure this can exert on us until it suddenly goes away, leaving us with a sense of tranquility and tremendous relief.

This is the key to understanding chapter 48 of *Tao Te Ching*:

Pursue knowledge, daily gain
Pursue Tao, daily loss

When we accumulate, we are in hot pursuit of knowledge. The acquisition of more and more material things ends up as clutter, which in turn leads to stress and agitation. In this mode of thinking, we put in a lot of extra effort but fail to gain any significant benefits.

On the path of the Tao, we let go of more and more every day. The more we discard, the better we can utilize what's left. The more we simplify, the easier it is to attain serenity and peace of mind. The wisdom of Ikkyu's story is inextricably linked to the wisdom of the *Tao Te Ching*.

為學日益，為道日損。

PART FIVE

At Night

深夜

Nighttime is the perfect time for reflection. One type of reflection is to look back on the day. How did it go? Were you able to apply Tao principles to achieve that combination of effortlessness and effectiveness?

Another type of reflection goes much deeper. It is concerned not with looking back but looking inward. What is the meaning of life? What is our purpose, and where exactly are we going? When dealing with such issues, it can be helpful to ask questions like the following:

- *What is our true nature?*
- *Where do we come from? Where does everything come from?*
- *Why should we cultivate the Tao? What is its value?*
- *What lies at the center of the universal cycles of creation and destruction?*
- *What should be our attitude toward death?*
- *How should we regard the afterlife?*

Chapter 28

The True Self

What Is the True Essence of Our Being?

自性

"Master," the disciple asked, "what exactly is the true self?"

The sage replied, "Ultimately, your true self is the Tao and the Tao is you."

"I find that hard to believe, Master. The Tao is great; I am insignificant. The Tao is powerful; I have but a little strength. The Tao is unlimited; I labor under many limitations. The Tao is everywhere; I can only be in one place at a time. As far as I can tell, the Tao and I are completely different. How can you say that I am ultimately the Tao and the Tao is me?"

Rather than respond directly, the sage handed the disciple a bowl: "Go to the nearby river with this and use it to bring back some water, then we'll continue the discussion."

The disciple carried out the order, but when he came back, the sage looked at the bowl and frowned. "Didn't I tell you to fetch the water from the river? This can't be it."

"But it is, Master." The disciple was confused by the disapproval. "I collected the water by dipping the bowl into the river. I assure you that this water absolutely is from the river."

"I know the river quite well," the sage said. "All kinds of fish swim in it, but I don't see any fish in this water. Numerous animals come to the river to drink from it, and yet I see no animals in this bowl. Many children from the village frolic in the shallows of the river. Well, I see no children here either. Therefore, this cannot be the water from the river."

"Master, it is only a small amount of water: of course it cannot contain all those things!"

"Oh, I see," said the sage. "Well, in that case, I want you to go pour the water back into the river."

The disciple did so with a puzzled expression on his face. He couldn't help but wonder what had possessed the sage to act so strangely. He completed his task and returned.

"Is the water back in the river?" the sage asked. The disciple nodded.

"Good," said the sage. "That small amount of water you brought back is now

the same water that touches the fish, the animals, and the children. In fact, everything that the river is now applies to the water we were both looking at just a while ago.

"Think of the river as the Tao and the water in the bowl as your true self. From a limited point of view, that water seems very different from the river. It is understandable how one can be led to believe that the two are not the same and can never be the same. The river is far greater than the bowl of water, just as the Tao is far greater than an individual human being.

"Having carried water from the river, you can now see it from an expanded perspective. The river is the source of the water, just as the Tao is the source of our true inner selves. You saw this for yourself as you dipped the bowl into the river, so you insisted that the water was the same even when I tried to convince you it wasn't.

"When you poured the water back, you saw that the separation of the water from the river was only temporary. It's just like that for the true self. Our physical existence is only a temporary condition. The eternal truth is that our innermost nature comes from, and ultimately returns to, the Tao. When all is said and done, we and the Tao are one."

The Tao
道

Just as the bowl contains the water in this story, we have physical bodies that contain our true selves. Having a bowl is useful in that it allows one to carry water from one place to another. Similarly, having a body is useful in that it allows us to experience the physical realm as a part of it.

Sometimes we identify with the body so much that we become attached to it and think of it as the self. That's like mistaking the bowl for the water. The water remains the same no matter what container it occupies. In the same way, your true self remains the essential "you" no matter how your body changes.

Just as the disciple learned a valuable lesson carrying water from the river and back to it again, we also learn from our experiences and various journeys through the material world. Just as the bowl of water is all by itself as it is being carried around, we can also feel alone and isolated as we move through life, working on our individual lesson plans. This feeling, reinforced by physical perceptions, can make us forget that we are all part of a greater self.

The bowl cannot hold water forever. It may be accidentally dropped and smashed to pieces one day, or it may develop cracks and break apart after years of use. Similarly, the physical body cannot last indefinitely. Accidents, injuries, illness, or age will eventually render it unusable.

The water must return to the river. Even if the water isn't poured back, but spilled somewhere, it will still flow or seep its way into the river. Similarly, when the body is no longer a suitable vessel, the true self it contains must return to the source. Religious people may call this source God; atheists may call it the laws of nature; we call it the Tao. Whatever its label, it is our point of origin as well as our ultimate destination.

Just as the water becomes one with the river, the true self merges with the Tao. That's when we realize that feelings of isolation and separation are illusory. You and I are never truly isolated or separated from the divine source of universal creation. We are never truly alone. Oneness, the Tao that unifies all, is the ultimate reality . . . of the true self.

上善若水

Chapter 29

The Seed

How Can We Say That Everything Comes from Nothing?

一粒種子

During the Tang dynasty, there lived a scholar by the name of Li Bo. He attained a measure of fame for being exceptionally studious and knowledgeable. Because he had read so many books, people gave him the nickname "Li of Ten Thousand Volumes."

In the course of his studies, he came across a phrase from the Vimalakirti-Nirdesa Sutra that he found puzzling. The phrase was "Mount Sumeru hides mustard seed; mustard seed contains Mount Sumeru."

It struck him as incomprehensible and illogical. How could something as small as a seed contain something as big as a mountain? It made no sense to him. Seeking to understand, he visited the Zen master Zhishang and asked for an explanation.

"One can certainly hide a mustard seed somewhere in Mount Sumeru," Li Bo said, "but how can a gigantic mountain fit inside a tiny seed?"

Smiling gently, Zhishang answered this question with a question: "People call you Li of Ten Thousand Volumes, right? So tell me, how can ten thousand books all fit inside your skull?"

The Tao

道

Just as the tiny mustard seed holds a huge mountain, this little story conceals great truths. We can explore these great truths through a series of mental exercises.

Thought Experiment

We start with the concept that something small can contain something big. For the sake of simplicity, we'll do without Mount Sumeru for now. Also, the seed doesn't have to be something as specific as a mustard seed. It can be a generic seed of a generic plant—let us say a tree of some sort. You begin this thought experiment holding such a seed in the palm of your hand.

Right away we can see that even in this pared-down example, the concept holds up quite well. If planted, the seed can grow into a tree. Therefore, it is quite true that there is a full-size tree hiding inside the seed.

That's not all, though. The tree that this seed can grow into will produce more seeds, and each seed will contain a full-size tree inside itself. Therefore, this seed contains more than just one tree. It also contains all the offspring trees that the tree will produce in the next generation. This can add up to be quite a few trees.

Next, we realize that there is no need to stop at one generation in our thought experiment. The trees can reproduce generation after generation, multiplying their numbers with the passage of time. Soon, there are so many trees that they can cover an entire mountain—perhaps a mountain as large as, or larger than, Mount Sumeru. This is a great number of trees, yet they are all hiding inside the seed in the palm of your hand.

There is no need to stop at one mountain either. The trees can continue to multiply until they carpet an entire geographical region (perhaps covering multiple mountains and valleys), stopping only when they encounter a body of water.

Even water is no obstacle, if an animal were to carry a seed across a river, or if a human traveler decided to take some seeds to another continent. The trees can bridge oceans; eventually they have the potential to turn the entire planet into one big forest.

Nor is one planet the final limit. In the distant future, when mankind terraforms other planets, the trees will bridge space to take root in alien soils and bask under the rays of other suns.

Thus, to be as accurate as possible, we need to recognize that the seed in your hand contains a virtually limitless number of trees within it. The total mass and size of this incredible amount of trees far exceeds those of any mountain. If a seed can hold the unimaginable potential for such a stupendous quantity, then holding Mount Sumeru would be easy in comparison.

Having peered into the far future, we now turn around to look at the other direction of time. What is the past of this seed? How did it come into being?

From its parent tree, of course. And this parent tree used to be a seed too. The same can be said for its predecessor, and the predecessor before that, going all the way back to the beginning of life on this planet. Where was the seed at that time?

Obviously, it did not exist as a physical object in the distant past. If it could be said to exist at all, it would be as pure potential. This potential expressed itself when the time was right, and manifested physical reality as the seed in your

186 · Derek Lin

hand—a seed that, let's not forget, holds a virtually endless progression of trees inside.

We started this thought experiment with the idea that something big can be hiding inside something small. Somehow we have ended up in a strange place, where we see that an almost infinite number of physical entities can come from the nothingness of pure potentiality. It seems to defy common sense, but when we look at the past and future together, we quickly realize that it cannot be any other way.

The Pregnant Void

This nothingness has many names. Ancient Hindus called it *Sunya*, the pregnant void. In his philosophical discussions, Bruce Lee called it *voidness*, or the *living void*. Modern physicists call an aspect of it the *quantum foam*.

This void is not an empty vacuum, nor is it the nonexistence of oblivion. There seems to be nothing within its emptiness, but in reality it is seething with infinite possibilities, all waiting to express themselves by taking form in the material world.

This is an important aspect of the Tao—without substance, without form, without shape, and yet containing all conceivable substances, all conceivable forms and all conceivable shapes. The phrase "In God all things are possible" is a glimpse into the divine genius of this supreme power.

Thus in chapter 4 of *Tao Te Ching* we see that:

The Tao is empty
When utilized, it is not filled up
So deep! It seems to be the source of all things

Having completed the thought experiment, we can now look at this passage in a different light. How the Tao can be empty and still be the source of everything may have seemed puzzling before. Now it begins to make more sense.

Everything comes out of nothing. Just as the source of all the trees in our example is the immaterial potential of the seed, the source of everything in existence must be the ultimate emptiness in the very beginning of time.

The Human Seed

This is a great truth that applies to human beings as well. You started your physical existence in this lifetime as a fertilized egg—the human seed. Like the seed of a plant, it doesn't look like much in the beginning. In terms of size, the egg is smaller than the period at the end of this sentence. But just as the seed grows into a tall tree eventually, in the course of time the tiny egg develops into the life-size individual you think of as yourself.

Just as the seed contains not only a tree, but also all the trees of successive generations, a fertilized egg contains not just a person, but also all the descendants of that person. In a dozen generations or so, this potential expresses itself as an army of individuals, each with his or her unique quirks and foibles. As time marches into the future, this army will continue to grow, until it becomes a virtually endless parade of human beings.

How about in the past? Prior to the beginning of your physical manifestation, you also existed as pure potentiality, just like the seed in our thought experiment. In that state, you existed as a part of, or in oneness with, the infinitely creative emptiness that is the Tao.

This is how we can say that you come from the Tao, and that the Tao is within you. The connection between humans and the Tao lies at the most fundamental level of reality. This explains why innovation and adaptability are such basic attributes of human nature. The infinite creativity of the Tao is mirrored within you as human creativity. Just as the power of the Tao gives rise to myriad things, you were born with the potential to reproduce and multiply, and also to invent and build.

This is also why Tao practitioners tend to be remarkably creative individuals. They are often artists, designers, writers, poets, musicians, dancers, composers, programmers, or some combination of the above. Those who do not follow these paths invariably express their creativity in other ways—the commonality is the importance of creative endeavors in their lives.

These people can feel their connection with the Tao. When they say the "creative juice" is flowing, they are tapping into their personal pipeline to the ultimate source. It is little wonder, then, that Tao philosophy resonates with them so powerfully. To these people, being in touch with the Tao is both familiar and comfortable. Others may see this sort of spirituality as quaint or exotic, but creative types see it as the most natural thing imaginable. The Tao has always spoken to them; they feel perfectly at home with it.

The Tao Seed

When Lao Tzu and Chuang Tzu wrote down their thoughts 2,500 years ago, they planted a seed. In the course of time, this seed grew into a tree with two large branches: religious and philosophical Taoism.

The Chinese did not regard the two branches as distinct and separate from each other. They tended to the whole tree. Their practice of Taoism mixed religious and philosophical elements freely.

The trees of Taoism did not develop as Lao Tzu and Chuang Tzu had envisioned. On the religious branch, Tao practitioners deified these humble and self-effacing philosophers. This was rather ironic, since they had never claimed to be divine in any way and probably preferred to remain out of sight. Their deification was, in many ways, completely contrary to the spirit of their words.

The philosophical branch did not fare much better. Somehow misguided quests for physical immortality came into being. They grew as twisted new branches that eventually withered and fell off the trees.

The Tao tree did not grow properly because the soil did not have the proper nutrients. Nevertheless, the Tao seed persisted. The potential within it passed from one generation to another, remaining the same all the while. Century after century, it waited patiently for the appropriate time to manifest its true potential.

That time came when the Tao seed was carried by human travelers into the Western continent. The Tao tree had bridged the ocean into a new place where it had never been planted before.

Something interesting happened. The rich soil of the Western continent had all the elements of nutrition the Tao tree needed to thrive. These elements included the rugged individualists, their ideal of independence, the freedom from artificial constraints, and a sense of humor—a perfect echo of the characteristics of the ancient sages.

Only a few seeds had been planted thus far, so society at large did not pay them much attention. Some people noticed the new growth, but reacted in different ways.

Some Chinese people looked at the Tao tree and thought of it as no more than an obsolete relic from the past. They had already stopped tending to it, so they continued to ignore it. They took it for granted and did not realize what a treasure it was.

Others looked at the same tree and noticed its remarkable elegance, beauty, and strength. They tasted its fruits and found them delicious as well as healthy. They looked around for books about it; they studied whatever they could find with great enthusiasm. Then they began to plant more seeds.

Today, delicate saplings are poking out of the rich soil tentatively and gingerly. They still have a long way to go, but at least they have taken root.

If you are reading these words, then the Tao seed has already been planted in your heart. You may have come across the Tao unexpectedly, or it may have manifested in your life out of nowhere. You can say that the Tao seed has arisen from the pregnant void to occupy an appropriate place in your reality.

Like any other seed, the Tao seed has unlimited possibilities inside of you. It may not seem like much just now, but there is no telling how it will express its incredible potential as time goes on. The question is whether you will allow the seed to grow into a great Tao tree, and allow the tree to multiply into a bountiful Tao forest.

Just as the mustard seed contains Mount Sumeru and Li Bo's mind holds ten thousand volumes, within your heart you possess unlimited capacity for the unlimited Tao. It is time for you to tap its power of divine creativity as you move through the barren spiritual landscape of the materialistic society of today. The seed of Taoism is finally ready, 2,500 years later and thousands of miles from its point of origin, to transform the desolate plains into the garden of paradise!

道沖而用之，或不盈。

Chapter 30

The Rock

What Is the True Value of the Tao?

道的價值

Once upon a time, a young disciple posed the following question to a wise sage: "Master, what is the value of the Tao?"

The sage gave an explanation, but the disciple didn't understand.

The sage knew that explanations conveyed by words weren't always adequate. The best way to cultivate the Tao was learning by direct experience.

He took a rock from his desk and wrote down an address on a piece of paper: "Take this rock and go to this address. When you get there, I want you to ask people how much they would pay for the rock. Don't sell it. Just find out how much people are willing to pay."

The disciple went to the address and found himself in an outdoor market.

There were many merchants hawking their wares and many shoppers browsing and haggling.

Beginning with the person nearest to him, the disciple held up the rock and asked: "Excuse me, how much would you pay for this rock?"

Most people ignored him and kept walking. Some glared at him. Some looked at him and sneered. Some laughed out loud. The few who did speak said things like "nothing" or "no thanks" or "go away."

After about an hour of this, a lady took pity on him: "Maybe I can use it as a paperweight. Here, I'll give you one yuen." She held out the money, but he shook his head and thanked her.

He returned and reported his experience to the sage: "Master, most people were not interested in the rock at all. The most I could get for it was one yuen."

"Good." The sage handed over another piece of paper. "Now go to this address with the rock and do the same thing. Ask the people there how much they would pay."

The address was in another part of town. When the disciple got there he saw that it was a jewelry shop. He entered and saw display cases full of glittering gems. Serious-looking clerks stood behind the counter. Everyone was dressed formally.

"What do you want, boy?" One of the clerks closed in on him.

"Uh . . . I want to find out how much you would pay for this." The disciple took out the rock. The clerk looked surprised, and then irritated.

"Where are your parents? This shop is no place for children. Out you go. Run along now."

I guess we're done, thought the disciple. The result here was no different from than what he got at the market. He turned to leave.

The store manager took notice of the situation. He glanced at the rock just as the disciple reached the door. "Wait," he said. "Let me take a look, boy."

The manager examined the rock. He looked puzzled, and then his eyes widened. He ordered one of the clerks to fetch the senior jeweler from the workshop in the back.

The old jeweler came out, grumbling about the interruption, but when he saw the rock, his eyes widened too. He examined it under the magnifying glass for a long while, turning it this way and that. Then he handed it back to the disciple and whispered in the manager's ear.

Suddenly the manager was all smiles: "Boy, I like you, so I'll exchange this candy here for your rock. Okay?"

The disciple shook his head: "I need to know how much you're willing to pay for it, sir."

"I see," the manager considered. "How about if I give you ten yuen? Is it a deal?"

"No, sir. I can't sell it. And now I have to go." He got the answer he wanted, so it was time to report back.

"Wait. I'll give you a hundred yuen. That's a lot of money. What do you say?"

Again the disciple refused to sell and tried to leave. Again the manager increased his offer. They went back and forth like this until the sum of ten thousand yuen was offered and turned down.

"I'll tell you what, boy." The store manager maintained the smile, but he was starting to sweat. "You tell me how much you want for it. Name your price."

"I can't sell it for any amount, sir. That's what I've been trying to tell you."

The manager had no choice but to let him go.

The disciple made his way back to the sage. He was puzzled. "Master, the highest offer I got from the market was one yuen. Now it went to ten thousand and beyond. Why such a big difference?"

"In general, people focus on external appearance," the sage explained. "The rock looks quite plain and ordinary, so everyone at the market assumes it is worthless.

"However, there's more to the rock than meets the eyes. It is in actuality a diamond of extraordinary size and quality. Only a few people have the ability to recognize it for what it truly is. The people at the market do not possess that ability."

"But Master, the clerk who wanted me to leave, he didn't recognize it either, and yet he works at a jewelry store."

"Being at the store is no guarantee of real knowledge. He probably knows the value of all the gems on display quite well, because they are all carefully packaged and clearly labeled. But when it comes to recognizing a real diamond in its most natural, unrefined state . . . well, he is obviously no better at it than the average person."

"How about the manager and the jeweler, Master? What makes them different from the clerk and everyone at the market?"

"The manager suspected the rock might be valuable, because he had years of experience with all kinds of precious stones. The jeweler had even more experience. He had devoted decades of his life to becoming an expert practitioner of gemology. That's why he didn't just suspect—he knew the real value of the rock."

The Tao

道

This story isn't about the rock or the disciple or the sage. It's all about the Tao.

The rock appears to be nothing out of the ordinary at first, but if properly cut and polished by an expert, the diamond within would stand revealed in all its sparkling glory. Similarly, the Tao often appears to be something plain and simple, but when a true master expresses or explains a spiritual truth, the Tao reveals its brilliant beauty.

The world in which we live is similar to the market, which is all about monetary transactions—haggling, buying, selling. The world is also an overwhelmingly materialistic place, filled with material acquisitions and price tags.

True masters of the Tao are few and far between, so most people in the world have little understanding or appreciation for the Tao. In the story, we see this reflected in the reactions of the people toward the young disciple. Even though the rock was in fact extremely valuable, people regarded it with indifference and even derision.

Chapter 41 of *Tao Te Ching* describes how different types of people approach the Tao:

Higher people hear of the Tao
They diligently practice it
Average people hear of the Tao
They sometimes keep it and sometimes lose it
Lower people hear of the Tao

They laugh loudly at it
If they do not laugh, it would not be the Tao

The three levels here deal with stages of spiritual refinement. They are completely independent of worldly distinctions like education levels, IQ scores, social classes, seniority, titles, and positions.

People who possess a high level of spiritual refinement recognize a spiritual truth when they hear it because it resonates deeply with them. In the setting of our story, such individuals were rare, and none of them appeared in the market.

Most people at the market were still a long way away from this level. They were used to dealing with things they could see and touch, like the tangible goods at the market. The intangible Tao, which arrived without colorful packaging, promotional posters, or a price that could be negotiated, was not something they could readily grasp.

There were also people who laughed at the Tao. These were usually the people at the lowest level of spiritual refinement. As we read Lao Tzu's description of them, it is almost as if Lao Tzu is talking to us directly about the people we have encountered who regard Tao spirituality as "weird." Some of them even express disdain and mockery: "Tao? You mean that New Age stuff?"

They look at the Tao that way because the material world is full of merchandise for sale, so people often mistake price for value. The easy assumption is that anything with a high price must automatically be high in value, and something with no price attached must therefore have no value.

This is exactly as the sage noted in the story, that most people relied on external appearance to pass value judgment. The rock looked unimpressive, so they dismissed it as worthless. Only the most discerning eyes could look past the facade and detect the diamond within.

If the market is the world at large, then the jewelry shop would be a religious institution, like a temple or a church.

In a jewelry shop, craftsmen cut and polish gemstones, and then present them in settings to be displayed for the buying public. In a similar way, a religious institution takes spiritual teachings, organizes and formalizes them, and presents them to the spirituality-seeking public.

The rings and gems on display at the jewelry shop represent the distilled and packaged religious doctrines we come across in daily life. The Ten Commandments, the Four Noble Truths, the Eightfold Path . . . They are commonly recognized and regarded as valuable, because they are clearly marked as such, just like the rings and gems with informational labels touting their value.

Oftentimes we have a tendency to assume that people in a temple must be knowledgeable about the Tao, but as we can see in the example of the clerk, this is not always so. The knowledge level of a clerk may be limited to only what he or she can read from the labels—the name of the product and selling price. Similarly, someone at a temple may know just the basic doctrines and little else.

When confronted with a spiritual truth, people at this level will have trouble recognizing it. They may even reject it outright without due consideration, as we see in the story when the store clerk tried to get rid of the disciple.

The manager of the jewelry shop represents someone at a higher level of understanding. Such a person has devoted time and effort into studying the Tao, and the extra learning elevates him or her above the lower levels, where people can recite phrases and rules but have no real understanding of the spiritual teachings behind them.

Although the manager seems to be the authority figure from the perspective of the store clerks, he pales in comparison with the jeweler. The manager knows a lot about gemstones, but his knowledge is primarily derived from gemology books and working with finished products. His foundation of book knowledge may seem impressive at first, but when he is confronted by something beyond the scope of his books, he must still turn to the jeweler for help and clarification.

The jeweler represents a higher level of understanding. He is the true master, because his primary source of knowledge is not books. Instead, he learned from diligent practice, working directly with gemstones from their most unrefined state all the way to polished rings, necklaces, and other jewelry.

From this, we can see that action is the critical element that separates a true Tao master from one who merely possesses book knowledge. True sages are not content to read about the Tao; they cultivate it through direct, hands-on experience. They must feel the Tao for themselves.

Just as the jeweler cuts and polishes gems so they can be made available for the public, the true Tao master studies, contemplates, dissects, and showcases spiritual truths so people at lower levels can easily understand the Tao.

And if we keep in mind that the Tao is simply a generic term for spirituality, then we see that great teachers from the past—Jesus, Buddha, Lao Tzu, and many others—are in effect master jewelers. They note the beauty inside an uncut block of gemstone called Spirituality. They can see this beauty, but most people cannot, so they work to bring it out in a way that everyone can appreciate.

The role of the master isn't limited to these great figures from history. For instance, there are many writers who can take great spiritual truths and explain them to us in a simple and fascinating way. They, too, are jewelers. When you read a particularly good book and it opens your eyes about life, you have come face to face with the work of a master jeweler.

What does all this tell us about the value of the Tao? The answer varies depending on the level of the individual.

At the lower levels, the people at the market could not tell you because they really didn't know. The clerk and the manager could quote you a price for any piece of jewelry you wanted to purchase, but they didn't really know the value of the rock either.

The jeweler realized that the rock was not less valuable because of its unrefined state. In fact, it was more valuable than any single piece of jewelry because he could create many diamonds of different sizes from that one rock.

This was the real value of the rock, but was this the real value of the Tao?

In the story the rock was never sold. Why not?

Because, as the disciple told everyone, it was not for sale. The sage alone understood that there was more to the value of the rock than any amount of money. The rock was not one of the goods that one could trade on the market.

From the perspective of the jewelry shop, it was associated with a certain figure that they would be willing to pay; from the perspective of the sage, no haggling, buying, or selling was possible because the rock simply had no price. It could not be acquired for any amount of money. Unlike all the rings in the jewelry store, there was no price tag affixed to it.

The Tao is beyond price. The Tao is priceless.

That is the true value of the Tao!

道可道，非常道。

Chapter 31
Creation and Destruction

How Can These Be Two Sides of the Same Coin?

生與滅

When you break something up, you create things.
When you create something, you destroy things.
Material things have no creation or destruction.
Ultimately these concepts connect as one.
Only the enlightened know that they connect as one,
So instead of debating this with your preconceptions,
Approach it in an ordinary way.
Those with this ordinary approach, simply apply the idea.
Those who apply it, connect with it.
Those who connect with it, attain it.

This easily attained understanding is not far off.
It all flows naturally.
To attain this state and not even know it,
Is what we would call the Tao.
To exhaust your mind trying to unify them,
And not realize that they are the same,
Is what we would call "three in the morning."
What is this "three in the morning"?
A man who fed monkeys with chestnuts said to them:
"Three portions in the morning, four in the afternoon."
All the monkeys got angry.
The man then said:
"All right, four in the morning and three in the afternoon."
All the monkeys were pleased.
The food and the quantity had not changed,
And yet resulted in anger and happiness,
All because of the different arrangement.

The Tao

道

This is one of the most well-known passages from Chuang Tzu, a sage second only to Lao Tzu as the most significant teacher of Tao insights.

The passage may seem confusing at first. "Create" and "destroy" seem to be completely opposite actions, but Chuang Tzu says they connect as one. How can that be possible? They seem as far apart from each other as any two things can be!

Chuang Tzu suggests that the best way to understand this concept is to use an ordinary approach. For instance, let's think about what must happen in order for us to create furniture. We have to cut down (break apart) trees in order to get timber. And what does a sculptor have to do in order to create a beautiful statue? He or she must apply chisel to rock and hammer away.

In both examples, destruction takes place during the process of creation. You cannot have one without the other. The two seemingly opposite actions are indeed the two sides of the same coin. By using Chuang Tzu's suggestion, we find that the paradox vanishes. We can easily connect with the idea and attain a clear understanding.

The monkeys in Chuang Tzu's story were initially angry because three portions in the morning and four in the afternoon seemed somehow unfair. Their caretaker, knowing how they thought, soothed them simply by switching the two.

To the monkeys, the new arrangement looked different and therefore had to be different. They did not realize that the difference was only superficial. Their daily allotment of seven portions had not changed one bit.

We can think of the monkeys in the story as us; the caretaker can represent reality according to our perceptions. Because most of us are as shortsighted as the monkeys, we often cannot perceive the fundamental oneness of existence. We see division and separateness even when they are illusory.

For instance, we cling to life (creation) and fear death (destruction) because we fail to see that the two are a unified whole. The process of life takes place at the same time that death continues ever onward. You cannot have one without the other.

If something has never been alive, it also cannot die. Death awaits us only because we are, at this very moment, gloriously alive. Without death, it is not possible for us to have this life that we cherish so much. Thus, life and death are but two sides of the same coin. Those who cannot see this are no better than the monkeys of the story, easily misled into thinking two things are fundamentally different merely because they are presented differently.

Those who can see it begin to understand why true Tao cultivators have no fear of death. They do not "conquer" death, for there is nothing to conquer or overcome. They simply accept death as fully as they accept life. Thus, funerals do not make them nervous, nor do they become obsessed about the hereafter.

They see the truth—that life and death are natural processes that occur at the appropriate time for the appropriate reasons. Just like creation and destruction, they connect as one and flow naturally. This is what we would call the Tao!

上士聞道，勤而行之。

Chapter 32

The Crying Princess

The Way We Look at Death

哭泣的公主

The Lady of Li,
Daughter of the Duke of Ai.
When the King of Jin took her in marriage,
She cried and soaked her sleeves.
But when she lived at the palace,
With the King slept in the royal bed,
And feasted on delicacies,
She regretted her crying.
How do I know if the dead don't also regret
How they at first struggle to continue living?

The Tao

道

This story from Chuang Tzu compares human beings to Princess Li. Prior to her wedding, she was completely unwilling to go through with it, just as we do everything we can to ward off death. Her tears represent our many attempts to extend life, remain healthy, and hold on to youthful vigor for as long as possible.

But once she settled into married life, the Princess discovered it really wasn't so bad after all. She got to enjoy all kinds of luxuries. Only then did she realize that her initial resistance was foolish.

In the same way, perhaps after death we will realize that the afterlife isn't so bad after all. People who have undergone near-death experiences report with remarkable uniformity that the other side is nothing to fear. In view of this, perhaps our mighty struggles to ward off death will seem quite foolish, too, when we have crossed over ourselves.

Chuang Tzu's point remains relevant today, 2,500 years after he put it down on paper. We simply do not know what happens after death. And since we have no information, why assume anything? Wouldn't it make far more sense to let go of worry and fear, and free up the energy to live life fully in the present moment?

富貴而驕，自遺其咎。

Chapter 33
Heaven and Hell

The Truth about the Hereafter

天堂與地獄

Once upon a time, a man with a certain military bearing approached the Zen master Hakuin and asked: "Master, do Heaven and Hell actually exist?"

The master wanted to answer in the affirmative, but knew that this would give the man a false impression. In all likelihood the man operated under the mundane paradigm that Heaven and Hell exist as places for souls in the afterlife. The master knew what he must do to break through that false preconception.

"What is your occupation?" he asked.

"I'm a general." This explained the military bearing about him.

The master burst out laughing. "What idiot would ask you to command an army? You look more like a butcher to me!"

This enraged the general. With a roar he drew his sword. He could cut down this defenseless old man in an instant.

"Here lie the gates of Hell," said the master. These simple words stopped the powerful general dead in his tracks.

Realization flooded in. The general suddenly understood that the master had risked his life in order to teach him a great truth in the most effective way imaginable.

"Forgive me, Master, for what I was about to do." He felt all at once gratitude, amazement, and shame.

"Here lie the gates of Heaven," said the master.

The Tao

道

This story tells us that even in ancient times, the sages had already evolved their spiritual understanding to a point where they saw Heaven and Hell as states of mind rather than places.

Not everyone shared this view, of course. We have always had vivid descriptions and images of Heaven and Hell from way back. A few enlightened beings recognized these as colorful metaphors, but many took them literally. In the cosmic scale of things, it wasn't that long ago that most human beings thought Heaven was actually somewhere beyond the clouds and Hell was deep underground in some dark, cavernous setting.

Specifics varied, but the overall idea remained the same. Asgard, Valhalla, Olympus, Hades, Inferno, Purgatory . . . all were places one might go after the death of one's physical body.

For many thinking individuals in the modern age, the idea of Heaven and Hell as actual places has fallen by the wayside. We still enjoy tales of the afterlife every now and then, but we don't necessarily believe that these stories correspond to reality.

At the same time, there are still many who do believe. Without too much effort one can still find people who simply won't let go of the notion that Heaven and Hell exist somewhere. Quite a few fundamentalist Christians, among others, will readily cite passages from the Bible to "prove" that Heaven and Hell are as real as your corner grocery. George W. Bush made news when he expressed his belief that those who had not turned to Christ for salvation were headed for Hell.

Some time ago a group of religious extremists protested in front of a Disney store in the Midwest. You may find this surprising. Surely Disney is as unoffending as they come? What could these people possibly complain about?

As it turned out, they were demonstrating against the action figures for the Disney cartoon *Gargoyles*. The main characters from this cartoon had batlike wings, tails, horns, and fangs. According to the demonstrators, to create toys in that image was equivalent to flaunting the image of demons and furthering the cause of Satan.

Disney employees received death threats and harassing overtures. The store manager was told, in a matter-of-fact manner, that he was destined to burn for all eternity. Apparently the demonstrators took the idea of Hell quite seriously.

In this age of political correctness, it is tempting to fall back to the "everyone is right in his or her own way" position. Can we not say that people like the above, who believe in a literal interpretation of the Bible, are just as entitled to their opinion? Is not their opinion just as valid as any other?

Perhaps, but as we look deeper we see that there are numerous logic problems with the literal interpretation. The foremost problem is that the horrors of Hell and the pleasures of Heaven are completely subjective quantities. What is horrible to some may not be so bad to others; what is wonderful or pleasurable for me may not be for you.

For instance, consider the case of a masochist. Does such an individual go to Heaven or Hell? Wouldn't Heaven for him be a place where he can sample a great variety of delicious pain? Wouldn't Hell for him be a place where he is barred from any pain whatsoever? Wouldn't this be a complete reversal of the typical conception?

Another problem, equally crippling, is the difficulty in reconciling the existence of Hell with the all-loving nature of God. If God truly loves His children, why would He subject even the most sinful ones to eternal suffering? Why not just settle for eternal imprisonment, without grotesque torture? Isn't rejection from Heaven and loss of freedom for all eternity punishment enough?

Look at our penal system. What do we do with our most heinous criminals nowadays? Often we are satisfied to simply keep them away from society; we feel no need to inflict pain upon them. Such was not necessarily the case back in a more barbaric age (or, admittedly, in some parts of the world today). At that particular level of humanity's development, society would not hesitate to torture prisoners, and many cruel implements were designed for just that purpose. Nor was it enough to execute a criminal; bloodthirsty sensibilities demanded death with maximum pain and terror—hence the Iron Maiden. This refers to the Iron Maiden of Nuremberg, not Iron Maiden the heavy metal band. Used as early as AD 1515, the device featured spikes of varying lengths on the inside of its cover. This cover closed on its victim slowly, so that the spikes would penetrate various parts of the body just enough to cause excruciating pain but not immediate death. The second shortest spikes were right at the eye balls, so the victim would lose his eyes shortly before the last spike drove through his heart, finally killing him.

Most of us would like to believe that we as a species have outgrown this hideous phase. Today we treat even the worst of the worst criminals in a humane way. If we must put one to death, we do so as quickly and as painlessly as possible.

Compared to our human-created system, doesn't a literal Hell featuring the most horrible punishment imaginable seem savage and primitive by comparison? If God is infinitely greater than human beings in every way, wouldn't His mercy and compassion surpass ours as well? If even puny human beings, imperfect and born full of sin, can rise above treating the wicked in a cruel way, then why shouldn't God, the paragon of perfection?

When we look at it in this light, we quickly come to the conclusion that if God is truly the embodiment of love and compassion, then He would never allow the existence of Hell as a place where sinners burn forever. It seems more likely then that Hell is a concept invented by human beings for the specific purpose of invoking fear in other human beings. The inhumane and barbaric nature of Hell is simply a reflection of the character of its mythmakers.

The key to this realization lies in thinking it through. People who still adhere to the old school are those who have not bothered to mentally pursue all the ramifications and implications of their belief.

When you do think it through, you cast aside the shackles of ignorance and savagery, and see the inevitable truth. Heaven and Hell exist within every one of us. That's the only way it can be. At any time we have the potential to experience either extreme or any point in between. We are not elevated to Heaven or cast down into Hell after we die; we transport ourselves there, and even though most of us don't realize it, we have the ability to arrive or depart at will.

Forget about all this eternal torment, everlasting pain nonsense. We are mature souls and evolved spirits who no longer need to be kept in line with scary stories. We do not need morality dictated to us and enforced with threats of punishment; our own morality springs from within, driven by our natural desire to seek harmony, love, and oneness. This being the case, our own conscience, higher selves, karmic lessons, and spiritual masters govern us in fundamental ways far more effective than fear ever can.

The sages were right about Heaven and Hell. Again we see how their ancient wisdom can still be miles ahead of—and sometimes even anticipate—our "modern" beliefs.

大小多少，報怨以德。

Chapter 34
Breaking Free

Transcending the Limitations of Book Knowledge

學以致用

Once there was a thief who had mastered the art of thievery. His exploits were legendary. His son looked up to him and wished to walk in his footsteps.

The son trained hard to practice the skills of theft, but he knew the training could not compare to the real thing. With the impatience of youth, he frequently asked his father to take him along on a heist, but his father always said he wasn't ready.

"When will I be ready, Father?" he would ask.

"You'll see."

One night, the thief told his son to follow him. Finally, the son thought, a chance for real action!

Together they moved stealthily into a large mansion. Once inside, the thief pointed to a door and motioned for the son to enter. The son went in and saw that it was only a closet. He turned around just as his father closed the door on him and locked it.

He whispered urgently: "Father, what are you doing? Let me out!"

Instead of unlocking the door, the thief went running down the hallway, yelling, "Thief! Thief!" Then he fled outside and disappeared into the night.

The son was trapped. Awakened by the disturbance, the residents of the mansion got up to investigate. The servants banded together to conduct a room-by-room search.

The son had to free himself, but how? An idea occurred to him. When the servants came closer to the closet, he made mouse noises.

Reacting to this, the servants unlocked the closet door to take a look. The son sprang into action. He kicked the door wide open and pushed the servants aside as he ran for his life.

Once out of the mansion, the son was able to get away. He made it back home, where he found his father waiting for him. "Welcome back," his father said. "Tell me how you escaped."

The son gave a detailed report. When he was done, he saw his father nodding. "Now you are ready to be a thief," said his father with a smile.

The Tao
道

This story is about an important transition in Tao cultivation: from studying the Tao as an academic subject to living its teachings as a way of life.

The art of thievery symbolizes the spiritual quest. The son's goal of becoming a thief is like our journey toward enlightenment. This journey can take quite a bit of time, so we sometimes become impatient, just like the son. We may feel stuck and wonder why we cannot progress quickly from ignorance to mastery.

The training that the son went through is similar to our reading of books about the Tao. Just as the son realized that his training was not the real thing, sooner or later we also realize that reading books cannot compare to actual cultivation.

While we can certainly benefit from reading, there is a gap between academic knowledge and the living, breathing wisdom of the Tao. There are people who read volumes of books and yet experience no significant change in their lives. Oftentimes this is because they are trapped by the words they read.

For instance, they may come across the teaching of *ziran*, or naturalness. The Tao follows the laws of nature, so we should also act from our natural selves. This is a great concept, so they decide they should also live in accordance with nature, like the sages.

But something is not quite right. They may show up late for a meeting or an appointment, and when friends ask if everything is okay, they explain that the tardiness is simply due to their effortless way of doing what comes naturally. They overslept, but that's okay, because they were following nature.

Upon hearing this, a sage would ask: "Which aspect of nature?"

This question seems simple, but it is not. Nature, like the great Tao, is all-encompassing. In terms of processes, nature offers progression, stagnation, and regression. They are all part of nature. Certainly we should follow nature, but which of these aspects should we follow, exactly?

In terms of evolution, we find development as well extinction in nature. Both are natural, so which path shall we take with respect to spirituality? Will we evolve naturally, or will we be naturally eliminated?

When we emulate nature without the clarity of this insight, we are likely to fall into the default option of inertia and whim. This is a path that leads nowhere, so we end up exactly where we started.

We can break out of this pattern by realizing that being natural does not mean following random thoughts of the moment. Instead, it means consciously aligning our actions and decisions with spiritual goals so they become easy and effortless. This is the key realization that sets us free. It releases the lock on the trap. Like the son springing into action, we burst out of confinement, push aside the obstacle of words, and regain liberty.

What we really want is not the freedom to do whatever we feel like at the moment. Living that way limits us to a level of spirituality we cannot transcend, so it is actually a prison.

What we really need is the natural self-discipline of the Tao. When we flow with this discipline and move steadily forward, we have the ability to, in time, take our spiritual practice to any level we wish, with no limits. This is the true meaning of freedom.

Having broken free, we are able to return home—to the Tao. As we look back on our escape, we can smile in knowing that, now, we are ready . . . to truly begin cultivation and live the teachings of the Tao as a way of life!

慎終如始，則無敗事。

About the Author

Derek Lin is Director of Tao Studies at the Great Tao Foundation of America, based in El Monte, California. He is an active speaker and educator on the *Tao Te Ching* as well as Tao spirituality in general. In his spare time, he serves as webmaster of www.taoism.net, a leading resource for the Tao on the Internet. He is also the author of *Tao Te Ching: Annotated & Explained,* an original translation that not only sets a new standard for accuracy but also has been lauded by critics as the first to faithfully capture the lyrical beauty of the original.

Lin lives in California with his wife, Janice.